W9-DEY-865

Losing Reality

ALSO BY ROBERT JAY LIFTON

Thought Reform and the Psychology of Totalism:
A Study of "Brainwashing" in China

Revolutionary Immortality:
Mao Tse-tung and the Chinese Cultural Revolution

Destroying the World to Save It:
Aum Shinrikyō, Apocalyptic Violence, and the New Global Terrorism

The Nazi Doctors: Medical Killing and the Psychology of Genocide

Death in Life: Survivors of Hiroshima

The Climate Swerve: Reflections on Mind, Hope, and Survival

The Protean Self: Human Resilience in an Age of Fragmentation

Witness to an Extreme Century: A Memoir

Hiroshima in America: Fifty Years of Denial (with Greg Mitchell)

The Genocidal Mentality:
Nazi Holocaust and Nuclear Threat (with Eric Markusen)

Indefensible Weapons: The Political and
Psychological Case against Nuclearism (with Richard Falk)

Home from the War:
Vietnam Veterans—Neither Victims nor Executioners

The Broken Connection: On Death and the Continuity of Life

The Future of Immortality: And Other Essays for a Nuclear Age

Birds and *PsychoBirds* (humorous cartoons)

Losing Reality

On Cults, Cultism, and the Mindset of
Political and Religious Zealotry

Robert Jay Lifton

NEW YORK
LONDON

© 2019 by Robert Jay Lifton
All rights reserved.
No part of this book may be reproduced, in any form, without written permission
from the publisher.

Requests for permission to reproduce selections from this book should be made
through our website: https://thenewpress.com/contact.

Excerpts from *Revolutionary Immortality* used by permission of Robert Lifton.

Excerpts from *Destroying the World to Save It*, copyright © 1999 by Robert Lifton.
Used by permission of Metropolitan Books.

Excerpts from *Thought Reform and the Psychology of Totalism: A Study of "Brain-washing" in China*. Copyright © 1989 by Robert Jay Lifton. Used by permission of
the University of North Carolina Press. www.uncpress.org.

Excerpts from *Witness to an Extreme Century* by Robert Jay Lifton. Copyright
© 2011 by Robert Jay Lifton. Reprinted with the permission of The Free Press, a
division of Simon & Schuster, Inc. All rights reserved.

Excerpts from *The Protean Self: Human Resilience in an Age of Fragmentation* by
Robert J. Lifton, copyright © 1993, 1995. Reprinted by permission of Basic Books,
an imprint of Hachette Book Group, Inc.

Excerpts from *The Nazi Doctors* by Robert J. Lifton, copyright © 1986, 1988, 2017.
Reprinted by permission of Basic Books, an imprint of Hachette Book Group, Inc.

Published in the United States by The New Press, New York, 2019
Distributed by Two Rivers Distribution

ISBN 978-1-62097-499-5 (hc)
ISBN 978-1-62097-512-1 (ebook)
CIP data is available

The New Press publishes books that promote and enrich public discussion and
understanding of the issues vital to our democracy and to a more equitable world.
These books are made possible by the enthusiasm of our readers; the support of
a committed group of donors, large and small; the collaboration of our many
partners in the independent media and the not-for-profit sector; booksellers, who
often hand-sell New Press books; librarians; and above all by our authors.

www.thenewpress.com

Composition by DIX!
This book was set in Garamond Premier Pro

Printed in the United States of America

10 9 8 7 6 5 4 3 2 1

For my grandchildren
Kimberly Lifton
Jessica Lifton
Lila Lifton
Dmitri Itzkovitz

We keep coming back and coming back
  To the real.

                              —Wallace Stevens

Contents

Author's Note . xi
Introduction: On the Ownership of Reality . 1

Part One: Thought Reform and Cultism
  1. Chinese Communist Thought Reform . 15
  2. Revolutionary Immortality . 34
  3. Ideological Totalism—the "Eight Deadly Sins" . 66
  4. On Cultism and the Larger Society . 94

Part Two: World-Ending Threats
  5. Aum Shinrikyō . 107
  6. Nazi Doctors . 134
  7. Trump . 152
  8. The Apocalyptic Twins: Nuclear and Climate Threats . 168

Part Three: Regaining Reality
  9. The Protean Alternative . 177
  10. Regaining Reality . 189

Acknowledgments . 193
Notes . 195
Index . 205

Author's Note

This book consists of excerpts from earlier work together with considerable new material. The excerpts are printed in regular typeface, while new commentaries are printed in italics. The introduction and chapters four, eight, and ten are new material but are in regular type because in each case they constitute a full chapter.

The excerpts weave together material from various parts of their respective books, and have been edited for clarity as well as for gender inclusiveness. I provide endnotes for new commentaries, while citations for excerpts can be found in the original work.

In the use of Chinese words, I have changed the original Wade-Giles romanization to contemporary Pinyin.

Introduction:
On the Ownership of Reality

I have long been concerned with those who claim ownership of the minds of others. And also with those who come to offer their minds to such would-be owners through whatever combination of voluntary self-surrender and psychological and physical coercion. I've come to recognize that the mental predators are concerned not only with individual minds but with the ownership of reality itself. I've been able to study a number of such mental predators, whether as leaders of extremist political movements or fanatical religious cults, or as purveyors of self-generated or solipsistic reality, as is the case with Donald Trump.

The general tendency among observers has been to identify two separate groups of mental predators. The first group is characterized by ideological totalism, an all-or-none set of ideas that claim nothing less than absolute truth and equally absolute virtue. A clear example here is Chinese Communist thought reform. The second group consists of what we generally call cults, which form sealed-off communities where reality can be dispensed and controlled. Ideological totalism suggests a system of ideas projected outward with the claim of providing solutions to all human problems. Cults, in contrast, turn inward as they follow a sacralized omniscient guru whose extreme version of reality dominates the minds of individual followers.

I myself held to that dichotomy until I encountered much that called it into question. I came to realize that ideological totalism and cultlike behavior not only blend with each other but tend to be part of a single entity.

I was jolted into that recognition by members of cults (such as the Unification Church) who embraced a particular chapter in my book on Chinese thought reform that described the psychological themes of ideological totalism. Beginning in the late 1970s, "Chapter 22" became a kind of underground document for many who were questioning or leaving cults because it seemed to express quite specifically what they had been subjected to in their own extremist environment. This strongly suggested that totalism and cultlike behavior are not separate entities but part of a common constellation.

Thus, totalistic movements like the Maoist version of Communism can include powerful gurus like Mao himself as well as sealed-off communities; and cults like Aum Shinrikyō—the fanatical Japanese group that released deadly sarin gas in Tokyo subways trains in 1995—can become notably totalistic and seek to impose their bizarre view of reality on the outside world. That is, totalistic movements are cultlike and cults are totalistic. In this book I will refer to that totalistic/cultlike constellation as cultist or cultism.

For instance, Chinese Communist thought reform, in its

many versions including its violent extension into the Cultural Revolution of the late 1960s, is a systematic effort at political purification of individual minds and a quintessential example of ideological totalism. But it also has included a deification of the person and words of Mao Zedong as not only a political but an all-enveloping guru. During the 1950s, and in the late 1960s, thought reform was applied everywhere in Chinese society as part of a vast inward turning in an attempt to form a purified national community of hundreds of millions of people. I was fortunate to encounter thought reform early in my work because it sensitized me to a particularly dangerous proclivity of the human mind for extremism, or what I now would call cultism. I have repeatedly encountered that proclivity in the destructive behavior I studied over the course of a lifetime of research.

Aum Shinrikyō, with its religious fanaticism and closed, guru-dominated community bent on spiritual purification, is the quintessential version of a cult. Yet from its beginnings, Aum's actions and behavior were intensely totalistic, and over time the guru and his followers sought to impose the cult's bizarre communal reality onto the larger society. Thus, divergent groups can be closely related psychologically in their shared cultism, their combination of the totalistic and cultic.

The excerpts in this book come from my earlier research and include work on Chinese Communist thought reform, the Great Proletarian Cultural Revolution, Aum Shinrikyō, the "eight deadly sins" of ideological totalism, the Nazi movement and the overall psychology of genocide, and Donald Trump and his followers. The destructiveness and violence described in these excerpts are fueled by intense cultism. A final excerpt on what I call the "protean self" and "protean-ism" suggests an alternative to cultism.

I will discuss some of the history of the word "cult" in a later chapter, but there is no doubt that in our time it has become pejorative. So much so that there has been a contemporary battle over terminology: "cult" versus "new religion." One can understand the insistence of many that, since "cult" is a derogatory term, the more neutral (though I would say, not entirely neutral) term "new religion" should be used instead. From as far back as the 1970s, I could hear the most articulate version of each position from two of my friends, each of whom I greatly respected. Harvey Cox, the venturesome and creative theologian, had considerable sympathy for many of the groups, even to the point of trying out their methods of worship, and insisted that fair treatment required calling them "new religions." Margaret Singer, the talented psychologist I'd also known for decades, wrote extensively about "cults" and their dangers. She had worked with hundreds of former cult members until her death in 2003, had become a leading figure in the anti-cult movement, and had to have special security arrangements at her home because of threats she had received from cultic fanatics.

I have insisted upon retaining the word "cult" for groups that meet three criteria: first, a shift in worship from broad spiritual ideas to the person of a charismatic guru; second, the active pursuit of a thought reform–like process that frequently stresses some kind of merger with the guru; and third, extensive exploitation from above (by the guru and leading

4

disciples)—whether economic, sexual, or psychological—of the idealism of ordinary followers from below.

Apocalypticism

In my work on cultism I have been struck by the significance of end-of-the-world visions, of apocalypse in the service of all-encompassing purification. That sense of apocalypse turns out to be present in extremist political movements no less than in extremist religious cults. Indeed, much of the fuel for the cultist engine is provided by a strong emotional commitment to apocalyptic world purification. At the forefront of such all-encompassing purification is a survivor remnant consisting mainly of members of the particular group, religious or political, making the apocalyptic claim. When Mao Zedong anticipated a nuclear war brought about by the "imperialists," the Maoist survivors would create a new civilization "thousands of times higher than the capitalist system and a truly beautiful future for themselves."

With Aum Shinrikyō, members' "mystical experiences" included images of the world ending and of a remnant of survivors consisting of the guru and a few followers. Aum also practiced a form of apocalyptic activism: of joining in the violence thought necessary to bring about an Armageddon that would usher in a purified world. That kind of "proactive" violence is always possible in a group strongly focused on a world-ending narrative.

Recent cultist expressions are a modern phenomenon that makes use of very modern components. Aum Shinrikyō, for instance, directly connected its vision of Armageddon with a strategy of recruiting scientists to construct the weaponry necessary to help bring it about. The assumption was that science could be enlisted to carry out the group's ultimate spiritual project. Similarly, political movements such as fascism and communism call forth their cultism by mobilizing their elaborate state apparatus and making use of trained professionals. Jeffrey Herf, a historian of the Nazi movement, has referred to the phenomenon of "reactionary modernism," by which he means the embrace of modern structures and techniques for conducting an anti-modern crusade. This could involve "great enthusiasm for modern technology and a rejection of the Enlightenment and the values and institutions of liberal democracy."

With the Nazi movement, the scientific claim was so intense and hyperbolic that a Nazi doctor I interviewed told me how he joined the Party immediately after hearing one of its leaders declare: "National Socialism is nothing but applied biology." That ostensibly scientific claim was, at its root, an expression of deep Nazi cultism, of the most deadly form of biological mysticism ever brought into practice.

There are striking parallels among the political purification of Chinese Communist thought reform, the spiritual purification of Aum Shinrikyō, and the biological purification of Nazi ideology and behavior. That biological purification, the essence of Nazi cultism, rendered the Nazis a genocidal regime. Genocide itself can be understood as the purification of the world by means of eliminating a racial, ethnic, or political contaminant.

In Aum Shinrikyō, the central mission was that of overcoming universal "defilement," and since the guru alone was completely pure, followers could only purify themselves by merging with him or becoming his "clones." In this way the guru assumes the role of a tyrant who has to be, in effect, "the last man to remain alive."

Owning Reality

That kind of purification is at the heart of the cultist phenomenon and is central to the quest for ownership of reality. As part of the imposed reality, the guru becomes the ultimate bastion against the evil of defilement, the central figure in the world-purifying apocalyptic narrative. That narrative is considered the only certainty in an otherwise unknowable future. That is, the guru becomes the sacred agent of a divine plan for all-encompassing purification.

Moreover, a guru can also claim to be the incarnation of a mystified "people." Mao Zedong, for instance, found another source of purity in his evocation of the always-pure "Chinese People." Similarly, the Nazis embraced a related concept of *Volk* that denoted not only the German people but their mystical essence. With the Nazis, the mysticism was biological: the sense of a great world mission to reclaim the purity of the Nordic race by eliminating racial threats to Nordic health and natural dominance.

Mental predators preside over these matters as part of their claim to ownership of reality. But what is the reality they would own? Reality is a concept that, despite centuries of psychological and philosophical investigation, defies precise definition. This is largely because reality is inherently paradoxical. On the one hand, what we call reality can be largely constructed by dominant social and political beliefs, as held by influential groups and leaders—the belief that democracy is the best political system, or that God exists or does not exist, or that human beings are weak and require dictatorial leadership. In any society such claims to reality can change and give way to competing and even contrary claims put forward by newly influential voices.

Yet at the same time there are more immediate, factual components of reality, which in no way depend upon such theoretical constructions. For instance, my father's name was Harold Lifton, and I am a Jewish American psychiatrist preparing a book of excerpts and commentaries.

Reality always contains these two contrasting dimensions—the changeable/constructed reality that strongly influences our worldview, and the immediate/factual reality on which so much of our everyday lives depend. We consider a person to be psychotic when he or she "breaks" with immediate reality in the form of delusions, hallucinations, and extreme paranoia. And we require a shared sense of reality, consistent with experience and evidence, for our collective function in a democracy. But we have learned that immediate/factual reality can be ignored or contested by people who may not be psychotic but who do so as participants in a cultist narrative of owned reality.

The Influence of Nuclear Weapons

The development of nuclear weapons radically altered the apocalyptic discourse. Now, we humans could make use of our own technology to do what in the past only God could do—destroy the world. This was the beginning of an era of human-caused technological apocalypticism. There has also been the fantasy that, since the weapons could do God's destructive work, they could also carry out his tasks of recreating the world and keeping it going. Here we enter the terrain of nuclearism: the exaggerated embrace of and dependence upon nuclear weapons, whether for "national security," keeping the peace, or otherwise enhancing the human future. Nuclearism takes us to the worship of ultimate destructive power as a kind of deity.

Various forms of nuclearism have been widespread among possessors of the weapons and those who aspire to such possession. The cultist mind is particularly sensitive to nuclear weapons and to the global destruction associated with them. Mao and Maoists were preoccupied with the weapons and expressed a wide variety of passionate concerns in relation to them: from the idea that all weapons, including atomic bombs, were insignificant in relation to the Thought of Mao Zedong, and that nuclear weapons were a "paper tiger"; to the celebration of the Chinese detonation of a hydrogen bomb in 1967 with dancing in the streets and waving of little red books of quotations from Mao; to the apocalyptic fantasy of a Maoist remnant. Even as the bomb was negated by Mao's words, it became part of a secular apocalyptic vision of political purification.

With Aum Shinrikyō, the nuclearism was more consistent. Its guru, Shōkō Asahara, was obsessed with Hiroshima and with the prominent apocalyptic influences of post-Hiroshima Japanese culture. He sought to make Aum itself a military power, by manufacturing chemical and biological weapons (which his cult produced, however crudely) and attempting to acquire nuclear weapons (in which Aum was fortunately unsuccessful). Both guru and disciples frequently invoked nuclear weapons in connection with the pervasive theme of the end of the world. They persistently spoke about Aum's great task of purifying the world following the nuclear devastation they anticipated. Participation in Armageddon-seeking military action was necessary for this highest of spiritual missions.

As president, Donald Trump manifested his extreme solipsism—his self-contained reality—in the form of a literal threat of annihilation when he spoke of attacking North Korea with "fire and fury like the world has never seen." As with everything else, Trump has been inconsistent and contradictory, declaring, after his meeting with Kim Jong-un in 2018, that the nuclear threat between the two countries was over. In the past Trump has repeatedly spoken of resorting to the weapons in various circumstances, asking why we would make them if we don't plan to use them. Nuclearism in any form is dangerous, all the more so when combined with erratic, solipsistic views and confusing changes in attitude.

More than that, nuclear weapons create a cultism of their own. From the beginning there has been a nuclear elite in charge of their construction, stockpiling, and potential use.

This elite is often referred to as the "nuclear priesthood," which suggests that its members possess arcane knowledge and mystical authority over the rest of us. Significantly, a number of people have emerged from this priesthood late in life and revealed to the world many of its secrets. No longer "responsible" participants in draconian nuclear planning, they could now give expression to suppressed doubts and guilt concerning longstanding advocacy of potentially world-ending policies.

We will also see that climate change has its cultism (chapter eight), much of it evolving around biblical accounts of apocalyptic weather events. There has emerged a cult of climate rejection resembling an actual flat-earth cult, and we are likely to encounter a great deal of additional cultism in connection with the extremity of the climate threat.

Zealotry or Proteanism

In this book, I look mainly at cultist behavior in groups and gurus claiming the ownership of reality. Groups led by gurus who claim omniscience can be particularly prone to cultist behavior. Where there is openness to the world on the part of a group, its leader may be more accurately termed a mentor. Mentors teach and guide and can provide followers with lasting truths without divesting them of their autonomy. But when a mentor creates a closed relationship with disciples that excludes all other truth—that is, seeks to own reality—he or she enters the realm of the omniscient guru.

I have also been concerned with psychological alternatives

to zealotry, and particularly with the mindset of proteanism. The protean self is characterized by openness, change, and new beginnings, and strongly resists ownership by others. While proteanism is most evident during periods of major social change, there is a sense in which it is inherent to the human condition. It has a special connection to the historical experience of modernity and postmodernity. I will say more toward the end of this book about the emergence of the contemporary protean self and of our capacity to resist attempts to own the human mind.

Cultism—like all totalism and fundamentalism—is a reaction against the potential confusions of protean openness. In that sense cultism is reactionary not only in its constraints on the self but on its efforts to stop the flow of history. Expressions of collective proteanism, one of which Václav Havel called "living in truth," can be viewed as a return to the resilience of the self and its dynamic relationship to the historical process.

Part One

Thought Reform and Cultism

Chinese Communist Thought Reform

Chinese thought reform was the subject of my first research study, in a sense my initiation into the realm of psychological history. I was fascinated by the process on two levels. The first was the individual experience of each Chinese or Western person I interviewed, which raised questions about the ways minds could be manipulated and altered and about distinctions between coercive and therapeutic approaches to individual change. These were questions at the heart of my profession.

But I was equally impressed by the larger historical spectacle of hundreds of millions of Chinese people subjected to a vast compulsory movement of "re-education"—in universities, schools, special "revolutionary colleges," prisons, business and government offices, labor and peasant organizations, and neighborhood groups. What was the historical significance of such intense political "psychotherapy" applied to citizens of the largest society on earth? I came to recognize thought reform as a project of political purification on a scale never previously attempted anywhere.

Indeed, I have come to view the thought reform process as

a form of psychological apocalypticism, of bringing about the "death" of all ideas and ideologies prior to those of Mao Zedong and providing a "reformed" remnant (in this case a very large one) to preside over further Maoist purification—of China, and perhaps of the world. I was studying not only individual change in worldview and identity but a grandiose and coercive effort at a historical "new beginning."

In that way, thought reform had a cultist element of Chinese society turning inward on itself. From 1948 through the 1950s, several thought reform–driven national campaigns took place, such as the Suppression of Counterrevolutionaries, Three-Anti, Five-Anti, and Anti-Rightist campaigns. Of particular interest was the "Hundred Flowers Movement" ("Let the hundred flowers bloom, let the hundred schools of thought contend"), which encouraged intellectuals to speak frankly about their criticisms of the regime. But authorities were surprised by what they had let loose, and turned the event into a trap. Those who had spoken out critically were subjected to fierce condemnation, with their position in society newly imperiled. Those initial criticisms were significant: one professor, in his response, said, "I find the term thought reform *rather repulsive. . . . I am not aware that there is anything wrong with my thought." And another put it into language I use in this book: "I think a Party leading the nation is not the same as a Party owning the nation." Such critics made it clear that difficulties can occur for those who seek to "own" human minds or reality itself.*

Yet, in the mid-1950s, at the same time I was probing these matters in my Hong Kong research, American travelers to Hong Kong told me about McCarthyism back home and its own assault on minds and on reality. Senator Joseph McCarthy and those who followed or were influenced by him were making wild accusations of Communist association against public figures, teachers, and writers. Subscribing to the wrong magazine might result in being fired from one's job.

That message, when combined with my everyday experience of thought reform's punitive distortions, gave me the sense that the whole world had gone mad, that there was a pandemic of assault on mind and reality.

Thought reform, then, is an extreme version of ever-present human tendencies to contrast one's own purity with the impurity of all else; and on that basis to justify one's claim to the ownership of reality.

Chinese Communist Thought Reform
First published in 1961

When confronted with the endless discussion on the general subject of "brainwashing," I am sometimes reminded of the Zen Buddhist maxim: "The more we talk about it, the less we understand it."

Behind this web of semantic (and more than semantic) confusion lies an image of "brainwashing" as an all-powerful, irresistible, unfathomable, and magical method of achieving total control over the human mind. It is of course none of these things, and this loose usage makes the word a rallying point for fear, resentment, urges toward submission, justification for failure, irresponsible accusation, and for a wide gamut of emotional extremism. One may justly conclude that the term has a far from precise and a questionable usefulness; one may even be tempted to forget about the whole subject.

Yet to do so would be to overlook one of the major problems of our era—the psychology and the ethics of directed attempts at changing human beings. For despite the vicissitudes of brainwashing, the process that gave rise to the name is very much a reality: the official Chinese Communist program of *sixiang gaizao* (variously translated as "ideological remolding," "ideological reform," or as we shall refer to it here, "thought reform") has in fact emerged as one of the most powerful efforts at human manipulation ever undertaken. To be sure, such a program is by no means completely new: imposed dogmas, inquisitions, and mass conversion movements have existed in every country and during every historical epoch. But the Chinese Communists brought to theirs a more organized, comprehensive, and deliberate—a more total—character, as well as a unique blend of energetic and ingenious psychological techniques.

When I began my study of Chinese Communist thought reform in the 1950s, the Western world had heard mostly about "thought reform" as applied in a military setting: the coerced bacteriological warfare confessions and the collaboration obtained from American (and other United Nations) prisoners during the Korean War. However, these were merely export versions of a thought reform program aimed not primarily at Westerners, but at the Chinese people themselves, and vigorously applied in universities, schools, special "revolutionary collages," prisons, business and government offices, and labor and peasant organizations. Thought reform combined this impressively widespread distribution with a focused emotional power. Not only did it reach one-fourth of the people in the world, but it sought to bring about in everyone it touched a significant personal upheaval.

Whatever its setting, thought reform consists of two basic elements: *confession*, the exposure and renunciation of past and present "evil"; and *re-education*, the remaking of a man in the Communist image. These elements are closely related and overlapping, since they both bring into play a series of pressures and appeals—intellectual, emotional, and physical—aimed at social control and individual change.

When I arrived in Hong Kong in late January 1954, I soon found out that those who had undergone this experience fell into two broad groups: Western civilians reformed in prisons, and Chinese intellectuals who had undergone their reform in universities or in "revolutionary colleges." As I immersed myself in interviews with both groups, I was fascinated on two levels. The first was the nitty-gritty experience I studied with each Chinese or Western person I talked to, which led immediately to fundamental psychological questions about ways in which minds can be manipulated and changed, and about capacities to resist such manipulation. Also involved were important distinctions between coercive and therapeutic approaches to bringing about change. These questions are at the heart of my profession and have significance for the way we live in general.

But there was another level to thought reform: its visionary or transcendent characteristic, the specter of hundreds of millions of Chinese people—in their neighborhoods, schools, and places of work—caught up in a compulsory movement of purification and renewal. What did it mean for such an extreme ethos to dominate an entire vast society?

As I proceeded with the work, I realized that one of the main causes for confusion about thought reform lay in the complexity of the process itself. Some people considered it a relentless means of undermining the human personality; others saw it as a profoundly "moral"—even religious—attempt to instill new ethics into the Chinese people. Both of these views were partially correct, and yet each, insofar as it ignored the other, was greatly misleading. For it was the combination of external force or coercion with an appeal to the inner enthusiasm through evangelistic exhortation which gave thought reform its emotional scope and power.

Coercion and breakdown were, of course, more prominent in the prisons, where brutal treatment that constituted torture was frequent, while exhortation and ethical appeal were especially stressed with the rest of the Chinese population; and it becomes extremely difficult to determine just where exhortation ends and coercion begins. I could observe that thought reform was by no means a casual undertaking but rather a systematic and widespread program that penetrated deeply into people's psyches.

I found it very important to consider what was behind thought reform, what impelled the Chinese Communists to carry out such extreme measures on such an extensive scale. The complexities of their motivations will be discussed later on; but it is necessary for us now—before getting to the prison experiences of Westerners—to know something about the Chinese Communist philosophy or rationale for their program.

The leading Chinese political theorists, although reticent about technical details, have written extensively on general principles. Mao Zedong himself, in a well-known speech originally delivered to party members in 1942, laid down the basic principles of punishment and cure that are always quoted by later writers. To overcome undesirable and "unorthodox" trends, he specified that

> two principles must be observed. The first is, "punish the past to warn the future" and the second, "save men by curing their diseases." Past errors must be exposed with no thought of personal feelings or face. We must use a scientific attitude to analyze and criticize what has been undesirable in the past . . . this is the meaning of "punish the past to warn the future." But our object in exposing errors and criticizing shortcomings is like that of a doctor in curing a disease.

The argument continues as follows: the "old society" in China (or any non-Communist society anywhere) was (and is) evil and corrupt; this is true because of the domination of the "exploiting classes"—the landowners and capitalists or bourgeoisie; everyone has been exposed to this type of society and therefore retains from it "evil remnants" or "ideological poisons"; only thought reform can rid him of these and make him a "new man" in a "new society." And long philosophical treatises emphasize the need to bring the "ideology of all classes" into harmony with "objective material conditions"— or in other words, to blend personal beliefs with Communist-implemented social realities.

In prison environments, Western civilians (and their Chinese cellmates) encountered a special penal version of these principles:

> All crimes have definite sociological roots. The evil ideology and evil habits left behind by the old society . . . still remain in the minds of some people to a marked degree. Thus if we are to wipe all crimes from their roots, in addition to inflicting on the criminal the punishment due, we must also carry out various effective measures to transform the various evil ideological conceptions in the minds of the people so that they may be educated and reformed into new people.

Penal institutions were referred to as "re-education centers," "meditation houses," or even "hospitals for ideological reform." Westerners spent most of their time—one to five years of imprisonment—essentially devoted to "solving their cases"; and they were not tried or sentenced until just before their release. The large-scale policy of "reform through labor"—the use of prisoners in labor battalions—was mostly reserved for the Chinese themselves.

In the penal institutions it was made clear that the "reactionary spy" who entered the prison must perish, and that in his place must arise a "new man," resurrected in the Communist mold. The environment did not permit any sidestepping: the prisoners were forced to participate, drawn into the forces around them until they themselves began to feel the need to confess and to reform. In all of this it is most important to realize that what might be seen as a set of coercive maneuvers, the Chinese Communists viewed as a morally uplifting, harmonizing, and scientifically therapeutic experience.

This penetration by the psychological forces of the environment into the inner emotions of the individual person is perhaps the outstanding psychiatric fact of thought reform. The milieu brings to bear upon the prisoner a series of overwhelming pressures, at the same time allowing only a very limited set of alternatives for adapting to them. In the interplay between person and environment, a sequence of steps or operations—of combinations of manipulation and response—takes place. All of these steps revolved around two policies and two demands: the fluctuation between assault and leniency, and the requirements of confession and re-education.

These physical and emotional assaults brought about a symbolic death in the prisoners; leniency and a developing confession were the bridge between death and rebirth; and the re-education process, along with the final confession, created a rebirth experience.

Death and rebirth, even when symbolic, affect one's entire being, but especially that part related to loyalties and beliefs, to the sense of being a specific person and at the same time being related to and part of groups of other people—or in other words, to one's sense of inner identity. In the broadest terms, everything that happened to the prisoners in these penal institutions was related to this matter.

In turning from the thought reform experience of Western and Chinese prisoners to the experience of "free" Chinese intellectuals, we arrive at the ideological center of the thought reform movement. Instead of being directed at alleged criminals and "imperialists," reform was used to manipulate the passions of the most enlightened members of Chinese society. They were asked to undergo it as an act of patriotism, as an expression of personal and national rejuvenation.

What had to be destroyed by thought reform was all mental life separate from or prior to the revolution, to be replaced by truly revolutionary mental life. Later I came to view the process as an apocalyptic cleansing of all the past—a *psychological* apocalypticism in which all prior products of the human mind had to give way to a new collective mindset that was pure, perfect, and eternal.

A national campaign began that was centered in universities (but including all intellectuals, whatever their affiliations), and included everyone from the elderly college president to the newly admitted freshman student, as "tens of thousands of intellectuals ... [were] brought to their knees, accusing themselves relentlessly at tens of thousands of meetings and in tens of millions of written words." Combining personal anecdote, philosophical sophistication, and stereotyped jargon, these confessions followed a consistent pattern: first, the denunciation of one's past—of personal immorality and erroneous views; then a description of the way in which one was changing all of this under Communist guidance; and finally, a humble expression of remaining defects and a pledge to work hard at overcoming them with the help of progressive colleagues and Party members.

The threefold Communist program was clear enough: break filial bonds, expel the harmful Westerner, and follow the Communist Party on the path to total redemption.

During the two years of Communist rule before this official campaign began, however, many Chinese intellectuals underwent their thought reform in special centers called "revolutionary universities" or "revolutionary colleges." These institutions provided the most concentrated of programs, sealed-in worlds in which thought reform existed in its own pure culture.

Many came to revolutionary universities in response to thinly veiled coercion—the strong "suggestion" that they attend. But others actively sought admission because they wished to adapt themselves to the new regime, or at least to find out what was expected of them; they believed, moreover, that a diploma from one of these centers would be a big help in the New China.

The psychological pressures at a revolutionary university closely resembled those in prison. There was the assault upon identity, although without physical brutality; the establishment of guilt and shame; a form of self-betrayal; alternating leniency and harshness; a compulsion to confess; the logical dishonoring of re-education; a final confession, elaborate and inclusive rather than terse; and an even greater emphasis upon the experience of personal rebirth. There were also important differences, such as the development of group intimacy ("the great togetherness") at revolutionary universities before the application of emotional pressure.

Generational struggles were, psychologically speaking, the crux of the matter. The orchestrators of thought reform recognized that traditional society was anchored in filial piety, and therefore put the overturning of parental authority at the center of the thought reform agenda. Indeed, I read of ancient parables sacralizing the practice of filial piety, some of which went so far as to describe the killing of a young child so that there would be more food available for one's elderly parent; or the cutting off of a piece of one's own flesh and boiling it in order to feed a sick parent. But from the early years of the twentieth century, Chinese student and literary movements fiercely attacked these Confucian principles. In the celebrated 1918 story "Diary of a Madman" by Lu Xun (inspired by the Russian writer Nikolai Gogol's story of the same title), filial piety becomes a literal form of cannibalism of the young, and traditional society in general is condemned as "over 4,000 years of a man-eating world."

The Chinese Communists considered themselves the inheritors of the twentieth-century assault on filial piety, and constructed much of their thought reform project around that assault. Their grandiose goal was to convert every filial son or daughter into a filial Communist. So all thought reform programs in universities and revolutionary colleges culminated in each participant's fierce denunciation of his or her father, as a person and above all as a representative of the evils of the "old regime" (the Kuomintang, a revolutionary movement that became corrupt and autocratic under Chiang Kai-shek, whose armies were eventually defeated by the Communists in a protracted civil war) and the reactionary traditional culture. In this way the Communists were manipulating feelings of guilt on many levels, and were demanding an obedience no less extreme or sacred than that of the filial son who killed his own child or cut off his own flesh and fed it to a sick parent. The reformed intellectual was expected to be, as before, loyal, self-disciplined, and obedient—now a filial son of the Communist regime.

We must still ask why it was the Chinese who developed thought reform. Other Communist countries have, to be sure, used elaborate propaganda techniques and various psychological pressures, but never with thought reform's meticulous organization, its depth of psychological probing, or its national scale. Nowhere else has there been such a mass output of energy directed toward changing people.

The very Confucianism under such severe attack in Communist China was, paradoxically, the source of much of the approach and techniques of thought reform. Confucianism had its own focus on "self-cultivation," involving criticism, self-criticism, and aspects of confession and re-education. And it was this lingering Confucian spirit that caused the Chinese Communists to make an ideological fetish of moralistic personal re-education. Confucianism shares with Communism the assumption that human beings can and should remake themselves, whether as a means of changing their environment, or adapting themselves to a changed environment.

Both systems always involve a subtle interplay between role and identity: one first learns the more or less formal requirements for thought and behavior, and only much later becomes in his essence the thing aspired to.

These traditional Chinese themes could be expressed in thought reform only because they were also consistent with Marxist-Leninist principles. And this double fit enabled the Chinese Communists to pursue them so energetically. Thus it was thought reform's combination of Marxist-Leninist, Confucian, and indirect Christian influences that produced the bizarre extremes I describe here: for when the Eastern notion of The Way was combined with the Western ideal of creedal purity, sincerity came to mean nothing short of absolute submission.

One other important factor in the Chinese heritage also played a part in the evolution of reform techniques: human-centered psychological skills. No other civilization has paid so much attention to the conduct of human relationships. The Chinese family, with its characteristically complicated inner maneuvering, has been an excellent psychological training ground: in order to be "proper," Chinese children have had to learn to be aware of the emotional currents in their milieu. And this personal emphasis has extended from the family into the rest of Chinese life: whether performing official duties or seeking personal objectives, the Chinese people have always put great stress on exerting influence upon the people involved—and there is only a fine line between influence and manipulation. These human-centered skills have been carefully nurtured over centuries, and emphasized at the expense of technical achievements. In this sense, thought reform is the modern totalitarian expression of a national genius.

But the spirit in which these human-centered skills were used in thought reform is certainly alien to the traditional Chinese cultural style. In the past, the stress was upon individual and social harmony; the ideal was that of quiet wisdom and unbroken calm. Such a cultural stress upon moderation, balance, and harmony—which we may call a "cult of restraint"—ensures a certain degree of preservation of self.

Thought reform has the opposite ethos, a "cult of enthusiasm" (enthusiasm in the religious meaning of rapturous and excessive emotional experience), with a demand for total self-surrender. It is true that thought reform implies a promise of a return to restraint, and of an attainment of relaxed perfection some time in the mystical Communist future, just as Confucius claimed that these ideals had existed during an equally mystical past or "golden age"—but enthusiasm and restraint, once established, are not always so easily controlled.

In breaking out of its traditional cult of restraint, while retaining its old penchant for the re-ordering of human emotions, China created a cult of enthusiasm of such proportions that it must have startled even the most immoderate visionary, Christian or Communist.

How did the majority of Chinese intellectuals respond to the cult of enthusiasm? Was thought reform really successful with them? What were its immediate and long-range impacts?

There were zealous converts who underwent a profound religious experience. They regarded thought reform as fine and ennobling and felt genuinely reborn, along with their society.

Zealous converts were usually youthful, either adolescents or young adults. Although they may not have been completely free of inner doubt even after their thought reform, their conversion was generally much more profound than that of the apparent converts among the Western prisoners. At the other extreme were the "resisters," those who felt suffocated by the program and considered it bad and coercive. But resisters who stayed in China could not, at least during the early period, reveal themselves; clear-cut acts of resistance were virtually confined to the few who fled. And the responses of those who did leave China led me to conclude that the program had been massive enough to make even resisters question their own attitudes and feel guilty for being against the majority.

The most usual response lay between these two extremes, and most Chinese intellectuals at the time could have been called "adapters." Adapters were partially but not entirely convinced by the program; essentially they were concerned with the problems of coping with a stressful experience and finding a place in the new society. Their feelings about thought reform may have been similarly complicated; they may have experienced it as painful, perhaps even coercive, but at the same time possibly beneficial—like medicine that may do some good just because it tastes so bad. Adapters, while by no means unaffected by ideology, were likely to be less affected by it than either zealous converts or resisters.

Beyond these individual responses to thought reform was the outspoken national response that occurred during one of the most remarkable of all the thought reform phases—the period of the "Hundred Flowers." In late 1956, the Party announced that thought reform would continue, but it would be a thought reform of a new kind: there would be "freedom of independent thinking, freedom of debate, freedom of creative work, freedom to criticize, to express one's own views."

When Chinese intellectuals finally spoke out, they bitterly criticized every phase of Communist rule, including Party infallibility, the benevolence of the Beijing regime, and the integrity of Mao Zedong himself. Many intellectuals said that their initial enthusiasm for Communism had given way to disillusionment. Some advocated the formation of genuine opposition parties, free elections, and other elements of parliamentary democracy. The absence of civil rights and legal safeguards was noted, and the regime's constitution was denounced as a "scrap of paper not observed by the Party." Critics also condemned Communist manipulation of information. And perhaps most important, many of the critics struck out at thought reform itself.

In response, the Party launched a full-scale counterattack. The regime was particularly sensitive about the criticisms of thought reform. It countered these with the claim that the Hundred Flowers episode left no doubt that more, rather than less, thought reform was needed, and promised the intellectuals that in the future they would be given thought reform "refresher" courses every year or even every six months.

The Hundred Flowers episode is important because it revealed that in a reform-saturated environment, there is the potential for a sudden reversal of sentiment, for the release of bitter emotions directed both at thought reform and at the regime that perpetuates it. Behind such a reversal lies the latent resentment that thought reform builds up in varying degrees within virtually all who are exposed to it. This resentment originates in a basic human aversion to excessive personal control, a phenomenon that I call the "hostility of suffocation."

Thought reform constantly provokes this hostility, first by stimulating it within individual participants, and then by creating conditions of group intensity that can magnify it to frenzy. In other words, thought reform is able to promote an emotional contagion—of resentment as well as enthusiasm.

One external condition that encourages the expression of this resentment is the release of environmental controls. This in turn leads to the breakdown of the individual's defense mechanisms, particularly repression, which ordinarily keep resentment in check. Thus, liberalization of the milieu can create a quick surge of resentment, which mounts until it is again forced underground by the restoration of a suppressive atmosphere. This leads to more hostility of suffocation, and thought reform is then on a treadmill of extremism.

Another limitation in the effectiveness of thought reform is its dependency on the maintenance of a closed system of communication and idea-tight milieu control. If information from the outside that contradicts thought reform's message breaks through this milieu control, it can also be a stimulus for resentment. But the break in milieu control need not come from so great a distance: life experiences within Communist China, outside of the immediate thought reform process, can also serve the same function. Thus, thought reform extolled the brilliance of the Communist Party's economic planning, but Chinese intellectuals, like everyone else, were suffering from shortages; thought reform preached austerity, but intellectuals saw a privileged class of Party members emerge. This kind of information is of course even more accessible to a thought reform participant than news from the outside world.

All of this suggests that thought reform cannot be conducted in a vacuum; milieu control can never be complete. The one-sided visions of thought reform are always threatened by the world without, a world that will neither live up to these visions nor cease to undermine them.

Communist leaders could neither achieve their perfectionistic thought reform goals, nor cease trying to; and every wave of thought reform made the next wave even more necessary. The stagers of thought reform were in this sense the victims of their own cult of enthusiasm.

A true picture of the program's impact can only be obtained by visualizing within the emotional life of individual Chinese people a fluctuating complex of genuine enthusiasm, neutral compliance, passive withdrawal, and hostility of suffocation. Overall, I gained the impression that thought reform served the function of setting the standards for intellectual and emotional existence under Communism.

2

Revolutionary Immortality

In the "Great Proletarian Cultural Revolution" of the late 1960s and the 1970s, systematic thought reform gave way to humiliating attacks on Party officials and others considered less than pure revolutionaries. Since the aging Mao was calling forth the very young "Red Guards" on a mission of "breaking and smashing," one could call it a grandfather-grandchild alliance against the parents. Certainly Mao was seeking to reassert his own control over the Chinese Communist revolution, having lost considerable standing from the harm his policies had caused Chinese society. But I take a broader view of this strange outbreak in focusing on issues of death and symbolic immortality.

Mao's mobilization of the energies of youth had to do with not only his own sense of impending individual death but his fear of the death of the revolution. He sought instead to bring about a revolution that was continuous or "permanent"—that is, immortal. That vision is expressed in the Chinese Communist slogan, "May the revolutionary regime stay red for ten thousand generations." The Red Guards called forth, mostly in the range of thirteen to eighteen years old, inevitably brought about great confusion and violence. And there was much contention between groups of Red Guards about who was the most genuinely revolutionary, who best embraced the Great Leader's call to revolutionary action. But above all, the atmosphere was such that, as one Red Guard put it, "So long as it is revolutionary, no action is a crime."

The Cultural Revolution itself was also a catastrophic expression of distorted thought reform and resulted in the deaths of something on the order of three million people and the suffering, it is thought, of as many as one hundred million. Because I published my book while the Cultural Revolution was still active, I knew nothing of these statistics, which emerged only from subsequent scholarship.

Originally, thought reform had been put forward as "humane," a process of re-educating people rather than killing them. But we see here how thought reform can also be deadly on a considerable scale.

Mao's own reality distortions had already led to a still greater disaster a decade before in the national campaign known as the Great Leap Forward. The campaign was meant to demonstrate Mao's conviction of mind over technology by substituting "backyard furnaces" for large steel factories. The building of thousands of these backyard substitutes led to a great shortage of agricultural labor. Cadres falsified or minimized crop losses in order to blend with Mao's visions, leaving the regime completely unable to cope with a severe drought in large areas of the country. This general inability to produce food led to massive starvation.

What resulted was an astonishing number of deaths, at least twenty million and probably even forty or fifty million or more, making it one of the greatest disasters in human history.

One could say that the Cultural Revolution was confusedly apocalyptic, seeking to destroy the existing claim to revolution on behalf of an obscure but fierce vision of renewal and rebirth. Bands of Red Guards exhibited a cultic quality as they formed their own communities in connection with the increasingly deified words and person of Mao Zedong. Mao became an absolute guru, speaking from a high podium to a million young people below. Though the behavior of the Red Guards could be hard to control, they were spiritually beholden to Mao's revolutionary charisma. Many became what I called "wandering zealots" in search of evil, against which they must "break and smash" and sometimes kill. Mao became a sacred figure, and the more deified he was by his young followers, the more cultist his relationship with them.

Mao's guru status extended to enormous numbers of the Chinese people, whether in the cultivation of reverence, in his omniscient "Thought," or in the ubiquitous "Little Red Book" of his aphorisms. Many of those aphorisms had to do with dying a significant death, which meant dying in a way that connected you with the immortal revolution. But the aphorisms also expressed the capacity of the Chinese people to accomplish the impossible, as the Communists had in their heroic military victory.

While the claims could border on absurdity, one should not be too quick to dismiss the assertion of a table tennis player (at a time of "ping-pong diplomacy") that Mao's Thought had helped him achieve victory in his matches. Embrace of a guru and his words can indeed enable one to call forth special energies and a sense of sharing in the guru's transcendent power.

But Mao and his followers could not escape the consequences of the inevitable falsehoods of a cultist group, especially as those falsehoods were turned into policy, as in the Great Leap Forward and the Cultural Revolution.

In the conduct of the Cultural Revolution, and of the thought reform process more generally, there is an assumption made about human nature. Mao spoke of the Chinese people as "a clean sheet of paper," a concept of the mind as a tabula rasa, or "blank slate," that is rejected by just about every school of psychology and neuroscience. Mao similarly assumed a "blank slate" on the part of the Chinese people in one of his responses to nuclear weapons. This was part of his own cultist apocalypticism along with a version of nuclearism:

> Should the imperialists impose such sacrifices [initiate nuclear war] on the peoples of various countries, we believe that . . . those sacrifices would be rewarded. On the debris of imperialism, the victories of the people would create very swiftly a civilization thousands of times higher than the capitalist system and a truly beautiful future for themselves.

There could not be a more apocalyptic—or mystical—vision than this futuristic imagining put forward by a leader of a secular political movement.

We recognize a sequence in Mao from brilliant revolutionary to cruel despot. This was documented by the man who served as

Mao's personal physician for twenty-two years, Li Zhisui, who paints an extremely negative picture of his patient that has come to be accepted by most scholars of modern China. Mao, often described elsewhere as an ascetic revolutionary figure, became one of the richest men in China from the sales of his writings, lived like an emperor, was served culinary delicacies, insisted on interrupting all nearby plane or train operation whenever he traveled, had attractive young actresses and dancers brought to him every night for his sexual pleasure, regularly transmitted venereal diseases to his sexual partners (despite protestations by his doctor), showed little or no concern even when directly faced with the suffering or death of others, and was frequently depressed and addicted to sleeping pills.

One observer summarizes Mao on the basis of the doctor's observations as "clearly a monster—egomaniacal, oblivious to twentieth-century science, technology, and language, paranoid, cruel, cunning, deceitful, and a sexual predator." These qualities, according to recent scholarship, hardly began with the Cultural Revolution or the Great Leap Forward: there were indications of some of this behavior as far back as the early revolutionary days in 1930s Yan'an. But they undoubtedly became much more prominent in the period from the late 1950s through the 1970s and continued until his death in 1976. What we can say is that Mao combined extraordinary revolutionary talent as a leader and theorist with late-life psychological and moral deterioration, completing a transformation from omniscient national guru to predatory "emperor," a sequence that has probably occurred in a number of other revolutionary leaders. Mao was both one of the most influential figures of the modern era and one of the most murderous.

For China, the Cultural Revolution could be seen as a last stand for ideological rectitude. After that, compromises were made, elements of capitalism were embraced, and communist ideology in general became more attuned to a science of power than to the inner meaning structures of Chinese minds. The Chinese went from cultist rectitude to large-scale official and nonofficial corruption. But cultist rectitude, as we shall soon see, has had a comeback in a new leader's embrace of Maoist cultism and cruelly expanded thought reform.

Revolutionary Immortality
First published in 1968

How is one to make sense of the extraordinary events that occurred in China from mid-1966 through early 1968 during the beginning of the Great Proletarian Cultural Revolution? How is one to understand the dramatic emergence of militant new groups such as the Red Guards, who at times seemed all-powerful as they pursued their campaigns of "purification" and vilification? The unprecedented and undiplomatic verbal and physical abuse accorded foreign diplomats? And the still more startling attacks upon Party leaders, along with general undermining of Party authority, including periods of violence and confusion of such magnitude as to suggest complete national chaos and even civil war?

I should like to suggest that much of what took place in

China during the Cultural Revolution can be understood as a quest for revolutionary immortality. By which I mean a shared sense of participating in permanent revolutionary fermentation, and of transcending individual death by "living on" indefinitely within that continuing revolution.

Central to this point of view is the concept of symbolic immortality I have described in other work: of humanity's need, in the face of inevitable biological death, to maintain an inner sense of continuity with what has gone on before and what will go on after one's own individual existence.

From this point of view, the sense of immortality is much more than a mere denial of death; it is part of compelling, life-enhancing imagery binding each individual person to significant groups and events removed from him or her in place and time. It is the individual's inner perception of involvement in what we call the historical process.

This sense of immortality may be expressed biologically, by living on through (or in) one's sons and daughters and their sons and daughters; theologically, in the idea of a life after death or of other forms of spiritual conquest of death; creatively, through "works" and influences persisting beyond biological death; through identification with nature, and with its infinite extension into time and space; or experientially, through a feeling-state—that of experiential transcendence—so intense that, at least temporarily, it eliminates time and death.

Applying these modes of symbolic immortality to the revolutionary individual, we may say that he or she become part of a vast "family" reaching back to what is perceived to be the historical beginnings of the revolution and extending infinitely into the future. This socially created "family" tends to replace the biological one as a mode of immortality: moreover, it can itself take on an increasingly biological quality, as, over the generations, revolutionary identifications become blended with national, cultural, and racial ones.

The revolutionary denies theology as such, but embraces a secular utopia through images closely related to the spiritual conquest of death and even to an afterlife. Revolutionary "works" are all-important, and only to the extent that these works can be perceived as enduring can the revolutionary achieve a measure of acceptance of eventual death. The natural world must be transformed by revolution while continuing to contain all that revolution creates. And the revolutionary's experiential transcendence can approach that of religious mystics, as a glance at some of the younger participants in China's Cultural Revolution confirms.

What all this suggests, then, is that the essence of the so-called power struggle in China during the Cultural Revolution was power over death.

In January 1965, a year before the start of the Cultural Revolution, the American journalist Edgar Snow conducted an important interview with the then seventy-four-year-old Mao. Snow found him "reflecting on man's rendezvous with death and ready to leave the assessment of his political legacy to future generations." Indeed, Snow's general description of the interview suggests a man anticipating, if not preoccupied with, death.

More important from our standpoint are the reminiscences that immediately followed—about family members who had died, about his career as a revolutionary, and about the "chance combination of reasons" that had caused him to become interested in the founding of the Chinese Communist Party. Involved here is an old man's nostalgic need to review his past life in relationship to his forthcoming death. That is, death is seen as a test of the quality of one's overall existence. And in the face of a threat of total extinction, one feels the need to give form to that existence—to formulate its basic connectedness, its movement or development, and, above all, its symbolic integrity or cohesion and significance.

Thus, for a man in Mao's position—of his age and special commitments—the affirmation of a sense of immortality becomes crucial. He goes on, during the same interview with Snow, to describe the two possibilities for the future: the first, the "continued development of the Revolution toward Communism"; and the second, "that youth could negate the Revolution and give a poor performance." The first is an image of continuous life; the second of death and extinction, of impaired immortality. Mao's ultimate dread—the image of extinction that stalked him—was the death of the revolution. The overwhelming threat was not so much death itself but the suggestion that his "revolutionary works" would not endure.

But why then? Why the crisis in revolutionary immortality? There is much evidence that the Cultural Revolution represents the culmination of a series of conflicts surrounding totalistic visions and national campaigns, of an increasing inability to fulfill the visions or achieve the transformations of the physical and spiritual environment claimed by the campaigns. The conflicts took on great intensity over the decade including the late 1950s and early 1960s, and found their quintessential expression in the Great Leap Forward of 1958.

The Great Leap Forward was a heroic attempt to achieve rapid industrialization and collectivization by making extensive use of the bare hands and pure minds of the Chinese people. Its massive failures resulted in overwhelming death imagery in several ways. It produced widespread confusion and suffering even as the regime was announcing its brilliant achievements. And its extensive falsification of statistics reached down, it was later learned, to virtually every level of Party cadre. This falsification represented something more than merely a conscious attempt on the part of the regime to deceive the outside world: it was an expression of a powerful need (dictated by pressures from above but by no means limited to government leaders) to maintain a collective image of revolutionary vitality that became, so to speak, more real than reality itself.

When the disparity between vision and experience became manifest, we can suspect that earlier confidence in China's revolutionary immortality must have been severely undermined even among those closest to Mao who had in the past shared most enthusiastically in his vision. Whether one attributed the Great Leap's failure to insufficient revolutionary zeal (as Mao did) or to an excess of the same, all came to feel anxious about the life of the revolution.

Maoists repeatedly called forth certain specific images to suggest the danger of the death of the revolution. These included "American imperialism," "feudalism," "the capitalist road," "bourgeois remnants," and "modern revisionism." But what emerged as the greatest threat of all was modern revisionism. For it is both an external danger, as embodied by a visible friend-turned-enemy, the Soviet Union; and an internal one of an insidious personal nature. It is a form of degeneracy or inner death experienced by those who once knew the true path to revolutionary immortality but, through a combination of moral weakness and shadowy conspiracy, strayed from it. Much more than the other negative images, modern revisionism loomed as almost an immediate possibility. The liberalization of 1961–62, following several years of economic strain and general unrest caused by the Great Leap and the corresponding split among Party leaders, also contributed to these anxieties.

Central to China's crisis, then, was a form of anxiety related to both the anticipated death of a great leader and the "death of the revolution" he had so long dominated.

The activist response to symbolic death—or to what might be called unmastered death anxiety—is a quest for rebirth. One could in fact view the entire Cultural Revolution as a demand for renewal of communist life. It was, in other words, a call for reassertion of revolutionary immortality.

A cultural revolution anywhere involves a collective shift in the psychic images around which life is organized. In Maoist China, however, it meant nothing less than an all-consuming death-and-rebirth experience, an induced catastrophe together with a prescription for reconstituting the world being destroyed.

The agents of this attempted rebirth, the Red Guards, revealed much about its nature. The tenderness of their years—they included not only youths in their early twenties or late teens but also children of thirteen and fourteen—was striking to everyone. After an official public "confirmation" and blessing from Mao Zedong during a gigantic dawn rally on August 18, 1966, the Red Guard took on national and international significance. Within a few days tens of thousands of youngsters with identifying red armbands were roaming through Beijing and, before long, the entire country, with all behavior profoundly influenced by the immortalizing vision animating the Cultural Revolution.

One must consider the meaning of the creation of a "youth force" at this time, and the specific functions it was called upon to serve. From the beginning the battle cry was the triumph of youth over age, of "the new" over "the old." Hence the Red Guard's announced early goal of totally destroying the "Four Olds" (old ideas, old culture, old customs, and old habits); and the similar stress upon smashing the "old educational system" in its entirety. The formation of the Red Guard was in fact closely tied in with a coordinated attack upon teachers, university officials, and educational policies, beginning at Peking University in May–June 1966. This focus upon education was part of an effort to bring about a shift in qualities of mind that were to be esteemed and rewarded. More important than newness as such (past revolutionary virtues were honored) was an association with youth and vitality. And the human targets selected by the young militants for mental and physical abuse were, in contrast, referred to as "old fogies of the landlord and bourgeois class," "the revisionist clique of old men (on the Peking Party Committee)," and, a bit later, as "old men in authority" and "old gentlemen who follow the capitalist road." The Red Guards themselves were heralded as young people who had "declared war on the old world." But in their attack upon old age and decay they were, psychologically speaking, declaring war upon death itself.

The special aura of the Red Guard could be attributed to not only its youth but its class purity. Its members were presented to the general public as an elite organization of youngsters charged with cleansing the entire nation, and one could be admitted to their number, at least during those early days, only if one came from a family of workers, of poor (or "middle") peasants, of revolutionary cadres, or of members of the People's Liberation Army. With the rapid expansion of the Red Guard into a mass movement, these standards were inevitably relaxed, but its purity was nonetheless constantly contrasted with the people in the "Five Black Categories" who were selected for attack: landlords, rich peasants, counter-revolutionaries, "bad elements," and rightists.

From this standpoint the August 18 rally that launched the Red Guard becomes a momentous historical occasion. Western viewers, when shown an official film of the event in Hong Kong and elsewhere, were so impressed with the intensity of mass emotion and primal unity that they compared it to *The Triumph of the Will*, the famous Leni Riefenstahl Nazi film of Hitler at Nuremberg. One of these observers, Franz Schurmann, noted the extraordinary dawn scene of a million people gathered in the great square singing "The East Is Red,"

Mao Zedong powerful in his presence though walking slowly and stiffly (and thereby encouraging rumors of severe illness), then moving out among the masses on the arm of a teenage girl. Schurmann went further and spoke of the formation of a "new community." I would suggest that this new community, in a symbolic sense, was a community of immortals—of men, women, and children entering into a new relationship with the eternal revolutionary process. An event of this kind is meant to convey a blending of the immortal cultural and racial substance of the Chinese as a people with the equally immortal Communist revolution.

On other occasions as well, the Red Guard could convey an image of young people touched by grace, bestowing their anointed state upon everyone around them. The general image was not unlike that of a children's crusade. They were a mass of youngsters unified by a transcendent vision, so infused with a sense of virtue as to be almost beatific—politicized "flower children" of the Cultural Revolution.

But the Red Guards also had another face. Theirs was the task of inducing the catastrophe, of (in their own words) "breaking and smashing," or initiating widespread agitation and disruption while spreading the message that this was what the country required. They became a strange young band of wandering zealots in search of evil and impurity. The Red Guard's symbolic mission was to "kill" virtually everything in order to clear the path for national rebirth, leaving only Mao and his Thought as the stuff of that rebirth. All this was seen as part of the general principle of "breaking down the old and establishing the new." But since only revolutionary Maoism was eligible to be designated as "new," everything else—especially that which felt un-Chinese, non-revolutionary, or simply non-Maoist—was "old" and had to be destroyed. Any violation became acceptable if in the service of the larger vision. As a Red Guard was once quoted as saying, "So long as it is revolutionary, no action is a crime."

The Red Guard was thus to embody and to demonstrate to all a principle of renewal and an image of perpetual youth—really, perpetual life—that was both revolutionary and Chinese.

A key to the momentum of the Cultural Revolution was the merging of purity and power. We may define "purity" as encompassing such things as self-denial (or even self-surrender) on behalf of a higher cause, the urge to eliminate evil, and ideological single-mindedness. And we may speak of "power" either as the ability to make decisions and take actions that exert control and influence over others, or as the sense of inner strength and capacity.

Purity and power are in fact psychologically inseparable. Both are ultimately associated with some kind of divine, or at least more than human, image. Purity is "godlike" and "god-given" in the sense of virtue so absolute that it transcends all personal frailty. Power is godlike in the more ominous sense of hubris, of humanity usurping divine prerogatives, and of a leader looking upon him or herself as a god. But, in a less pejorative sense, power is god-given because it is attributed either to an immortal legacy—the Mandate of Heaven or Divine

Right of Kings—or to an individual "gift" for ruling a nation that is virtually superhuman.

Interwoven themes of power and purity are therefore likely to dominate any collective quest for transcendence. They readily give rise to forms of ideological totalism that were so prominent in the Chinese Revolution. And the accompanying polarization of good and evil leads to distinctions between "people" and "nonpeople," to decisions concerning which groups are entitled to exist and which are not, or to what I have called the "dispensing of existence"—all in the name of superior virtue. Power becomes the harnessing of purity for an immortal quest.

Mao's misgivings about his revolutionary heirs concern their capacity to maintain a proper combination of purity and power. And his fearful image of the "death of the revolution" is one of breakdown of that combination, with disintegration of both elements. The Red Guards were mobilized to confront this breakdown by simultaneously seizing power for the Maoists and transforming ubiquitous contamination into all-consuming purity.

In the delineation of purity, great stress was placed upon what could be considered rural and "Chinese" as opposed to the threatening impurities of the urban and the foreign. Here we sense a restorationist impulse, the Maoist attempt to recapture a form of harmony (purity) felt to exist in the past among people close to the earth until they were "contaminated" by the complexities of modern existence.

———

To further understand how Mao blended purity and power, we must understand that remarkable entity, the Thought of Mao Zedong. The man and his words fused into a powerful image, which became the essence of revolutionary immortality as well as the energizer for its quest.

This was by no means the first time that a political leader was made into a divinity. But few in the past could have matched Mao in the superlatives used, the number of celebrants, or the thoroughness with which the message of glory has been disseminated. Even more unique was the way in which the leader's words became vehicles for elevating him, during his lifetime, to a place above that of the state itself or its institutional source of purity and power, in this case the Party.

In Mao's writing is a characteristic quality of tone and content that, more than any other, shaped the psychic contours of the Cultural Revolution. I refer to a kind of existential absolute, an insistence upon all-or-none confrontation with death. Mao always further insists that the confrontation be rendered meaningful, that it be associated with a mode of transcendence. This quality of thought is amply illustrated by many selections contained in the little red bible of the Cultural Revolution, *Quotations from Chairman Mao Zedong*.

A leader who can instill transcendent principles in his followers can turn the most extreme threat and disintegration into an ordered certainty of mission, and convert the most incapacitating death anxiety into a death-conquering calm of near-invincibility. He can in fact become the omnipotent guide sought by all totalist movements—precisely the meaning of the characterization of Mao during the Cultural Revolution as the "Great Leader, Great Teacher, Great Supreme Commander, and Great Helmsman." The Thought of Mao became not so much an exact blueprint for the future as a "Way," a call to a particular mode of being on behalf of a transcendent purpose.

Behind this Way were two psychological assumptions long prominent in Mao's Thought but never so overtly insisted upon as during the Cultural Revolution. The first was an image of the human mind as infinitely malleable, capable of being reformed, transformed, and rectified without limit. The second was a related vision of the will as all-powerful, even to the extent that (in his own words) "the subjective creates the objective." That is, man's capacity for both undergoing change and changing his environment is unlimited; once he makes the decision for change, the entire universe can be bent to his will. But again, the controlling image is the sense of revolutionary immortality that confers these vaulting capacities upon the mind. And the key to psychic malleability and power—the central purpose of the thought reform process— is the replacement of prior modes of immortality (especially the biological one provided by the Chinese family system) with the newer revolutionary modes: those of the biosocial revolutionary "Family," of enduring revolutionary "works," and of transcendent revolutionary enthusiasm.

The Cultural Revolution concretized this entire process, so that Mao the man and the "Thought of Mao Tse-tung" converged in an immortalizing corpus. Mao came to be regularly described in the Chinese press as "the greatest genius today," and all were assured that "where the thought of Mao Tse-tung shines, there people see the way to fight for their liberation and there is hope for the victory of revolution." Also highly significant was the merging of this man-thought corpus with the larger immortal cultural-revolutionary substance we have spoken of, the merging of Mao with "the masses."

Mao's Thought itself was sacralized—spoken of as "a compass and spiritual food" of which "every word . . . is as good as ten thousand words." And this sacred quality of Maoist thought was in turn directly associated with the desired revolutionary totalism.

The total revolutionary was "ready to sacrifice his life" and was "not . . . afraid of wolves ahead and tigers behind . . . determined to change heaven and earth, fight the enemy, stick to the truth." Such dedication and courage were indeed possible insofar as one could genuinely worship Mao's Thought along lines suggested in the following passage, which could well be viewed as the epitome of the immortalization of the word and all who embraced it:

The thought of Mao Tse-tung is the sun in our heart, is the root of our life, is the source of all our strength. Through this, man becomes unselfish, daring, intelligent, able to do everything; he is not conquered by any difficulty and can conquer every enemy. The thought of Mao Tse-tung transforms man's ideology, transforms the Fatherland . . . through this the oppressed people of the world will rise.

The Maoist corpus was elevated to an all-consuming prophecy: it nurtured men, predicted their future, and changed the world to accomplish its own prediction; it set in motion spiritual forces against which nothing could stand.

During the Cultural Revolution, the thoughts of Mao were claimed to be responsible for China's brilliant successes in international table tennis competition as well as for such large tasks as the drilling of oil wells, the construction of great modern airports, the completion in record time of the highly advanced and elaborate equipment for the steel industry, and the unexpectedly early completion and successful testing of a hydrogen bomb (in June 1967). Who is to say that none of the technicians and soldiers later praised for their courageous achievements in entering the test area to evaluate the bomb's effects were sustained at all by the death-defying Maoist images we have discussed? The slogan used on that occasion—"When men listen to this Chairman, machinery listens to men"—can become a dangerous simplification for a regime bent on industrialization. Indeed, as we shall soon observe, the entire Maoist program foundered on it. All the same, men in a variety of situations could feel themselves strengthened by allying themselves to such an immortal corpus.

But it was in the nature of the Maoist corpus—child that it was of the excesses of the Cultural Revolution—to overstep itself and move toward an ideological abyss, as suggested in a statement by the Communist military and political leader Lin Biao: "The best weapon of our troops is not the airplane, cannon, tank, or atomic bomb, but the thought of Mao

Tse-tung; the greatest fighting force is the man armed with the thought of Mao Tse-tung, daring, not afraid of death." In the same spirit, Mao's Thought was said to articulate the "final struggle" between the world's "two major forces, revolution and counter-revolution." It was held to be the key to the "revolutionization of man," the inspiration for "the heroes [who] have aptly said: 'We must live for the people and die for the people . . . a revolutionary has no fear of death and one who fears death is no revolutionary.'" Now the message was: so powerful has the immortal corpus rendered us that we become absolute conquerors of men, technology, and death.

One might be tempted to dismiss the entire cult of Mao and his Thought as no more than sycophantic indulgence of an old man's vanity were it not for the life Mao lived and the impact he made upon the Chinese people. No twentieth-century life has come closer than his to the great myth of the hero—with its "road of trials," or prolonged encounter with death, and its mastery of that encounter in a way that enhances the life of one's people.

His message of mastery over death anxiety was reinforced by his personal legend, which included fighting in many battles, being pronounced dead on several occasions, and being captured and escaping from enemy troops. His story took on special relevance for a people living through a period (the first half of the twentieth century) in which anxiety was continuously mobilized by extreme dislocation, violence, and loss. During such times there is always a hunger for words and acts that contribute to the re-ordering and "re-symbolization" of collective existence.

Mao's relationship to the myth of the hero was also enhanced by certain qualities of personal and revolutionary style that reveal a man closely attuned to the pulse of immortality. One such trait was his celebrated "revolutionary romanticism," a designation that would sound highly derogatory to most Communist ears but which official Chinese commentaries have associated with courage in the face of objective difficulties, and with great revolutionary vision (to be distinguished, of course, from non-revolutionary romanticism, regarded as an unrealistic expression of philosophical idealism). Mao's revolutionary romanticism, then, was the hero's quest for doing more than the possible, risking and even courting death in order to alter the meaning of both life and death, "storming heaven" and challenging the claims of existing deities, political as well as theological, in order to replace them with the claims of revolutionary immortality.

A closely related psychological and historical pattern was his extreme identification with what has been called his "mystical faith" in the Chinese rural masses. It was clear that from the time of his youth Mao felt himself deeply involved in a struggle to restore national pride—which over the years became nothing less than a heroic quest to reassert the life-power of China. Hence, Mao came to associate communism with the timeless virtues of the peasant masses and of the Chinese earth. And his relentless pursuit of the thought reform process was an effort to cement this association, especially within the minds of intellectuals. Mao once described his Communist movement as "passionately concerned with the fate of the Chinese nation, and moreover with its fate throughout all eternity." Rather than speak of Mao as a "father figure" or "mother figure" for his countrymen (no doubt he was both), we do better to see him as a death-conquering hero who became the embodiment of Chinese immortality.

Over the course of Mao's later career, the word becomes not only flesh but his flesh. The man-word corpus is increasingly represented as absolutely identical with China's destiny. And we sense that we are witnessing the tragic transition from the Great Leader to the despot.

Mao's active participation in the creation of his own cult became increasingly clear. His rewriting of earlier works—in order, as Stuart Schram says, "to remove both youthful errors and any points of fact or doctrine which did not suit the current orthodoxy"—was consistent with practices of other modern Communist leaders, and also with those of premodern Chinese emperors in the process of enthroning themselves and establishing new dynasties.

But Mao seemed to go further than anyone else in the infusion of his man-word corpus into every psychological cranny of Chinese existence. So involved did he become with the principle of the cult of the leader that much of his anger toward Nikita Khrushchev was believed to be bound up with the latter's policy of de-Stalinization and accompanying theoretical attack upon the "cult of personality" in general. Thus, when Edgar Snow observed (during his 1965 interview with Mao) that China had been criticized for fostering such a cult, Mao admitted that "perhaps there was some." Mao then pointed out that Stalin had been the center of a cult of personality, and asked in turn whether it was possible that Khrushchev fell "because he had no cult of personality at all."

Mao apparently required the immortalizing corpus for his "romantic" sense of self and history, his image of heroic confrontation with the powers of heaven and earth. The extremities of the deification would seem to confirm his highly active complicity in the process, and his loss of perspective concerning its wider impact. The image of Mao became almost literally a deity. And the attendant stress upon "Chairman Mao's good health and long life" seemed to make him into a kind of legendary hero who had achieved something close to physical omnipotence and immortality of the flesh. And most significant of all was the godlike style of Mao's participation in public events—such as the great Red Guard rally of August 18, 1966, at which he emerged at sunrise, a silent divinity who witnessed everything and by his mere presence conferred upon hundreds of thousands (on other occasions, millions) of young people a sense of being reawakened in purity—much in the manner of an Indian holy man who need only make an appearance before ordinary people to transmit his godlike power to them.

But the Great Leader turns into a despot when he loses confidence in his claim to immortality. Then, feeling himself threatened by biological and symbolic death, he becomes obsessed with survival as such. He is no longer able to put his death guilt effectively in the service of a noble mission, and instead becomes an "eternal survivor" who requires the defeat or death of a never-ending series of "enemies" in order to reactivate his own life and revive his ever faltering sense of immortality. He depends heavily upon the mechanism of denial—upon the fantasy of, "I am not losing my power, I am not dying."

Mao resorted to ever more desperate and magical efforts at achieving vitality. Involved here was an old man's fear that he was losing his potency, the special power of one who has felt himself to be a transmitter of forces shaping the destiny of humankind.

Threatened by loss of personal and revolutionary power, he sought to revitalize himself through a reassertion of purity and sought to buttress a relationship to the eternal by calling upon the purity and life-power of the young. Mao enlarged his quest for purity to include the whole of China and staked the future of an entire revolution upon it. Thus the bold stroke of a leader's genius became the despotic turbulence of an eternal survivor.

This led to Mao's plunge into psychism, into one-sided focus upon intra-psychic purity at the expense of extra-psychic reality. In place of his formerly sensitive application of personal passions to China's desperate historical experience, we encounter instead a misplaced faith in his own psychic state—a substitution of his own psychic history for history at large. Because he and a few around him feared the death of the revolution, China had to be made to convulse.

Each Chinese person—really, humanity itself—was a tabula rasa, a "clean sheet of paper" upon which anything could be written. By imprinting upon one's mind "the newest and most beautiful words" and "the newest and most beautiful pictures," all problems of the inner and outer worlds could be solved. This is the essence of psychism. The leader turns inward toward an increasingly idiosyncratic and extreme vision of immortality, and demands that his vision be permanently imprinted upon all. Mao's actions belied his stated willingness to leave assessments of present revolutionary developments to future generations. As much as any leader in recent centuries he sought to chart and control history and "fix its course for centuries to come." The more resistance to this course he encountered among the living, the more he looked toward the infinity of the future and sought vindication from the unborn.

The phenomenon of psychism, then, was a key to the limitations of the Maoist vision. And psychism is closely bound up with technology—with the distinction humans must make between self and things, between mind and its material products. It is not surprising that psychism of various kinds emerged very strongly during the movement epitomizing Mao's confrontation with technology, the Great Leap Forward. The "beautiful words" and "beautiful pictures" he then envisioned being written and painted on a "blank" Chinese people were words and pictures of rapid technological achievement. His assumption was that China "might not need as much time as previously thought to catch up with the big capitalist countries in industrial and agricultural production." Equally significant was the simultaneous emergence of the slogan of the "uninterrupted" or "permanent" revolution, a slogan which can be understood as an ideological call to revolutionary immortality, and which paved the way for the Cultural Revolution.

Here we see in operation the Maoist assumption that "revolutionary enthusiasm and ideological purity could make up for the lack of technical competence and material means." We are dealing then with a psychistic fallacy, an assumption of the interchangeability of psychic state and technology. Technology was sought but feelings were cultivated. The feeling-state could, in fact, become the entire operative universe. And that psychic state became interchangeable not only with technology but with nature itself. There was no external world, only a struggle for internal perfection. Subjected to intense methods of psychological influence, an entire nation was asked to treat the physical universe as if it were nothing but feeling and will. In the process of attempting to subjugate technology and nature to human control (or "to subjective capacities"), their material actuality was denied. The consequences of this psychistic fallacy could not remain hidden; they were in fact a major cause of opposition to Mao among formerly loyal followers.

Maoist dilemmas around technology and psychism arose also in the Faustian realm of nuclear weapons, with Mao's highly revealing way of responding to this revolution in destructive technology: rather than tell his followers that the world itself has changed—or that humans' relationship to death and life has altered—Mao instead exhorted them to renew their intra-psychic efforts at purification. Here were the beginnings of a nuclear psychism that later emerged so prominently in Mao's Thought. We can sense that Maoist psychism concerning nuclear weapons, as elsewhere, was intimately bound up with the fear of the death of the Chinese Revolution.

Everything about the Cultural Revolution renders one humble. I refer partly to the surprise with which it burst upon the world and to its continuing unpredictability. There was also its strange combination of futuristic tone and aura of the past. In many ways the Cultural Revolution was a "last stand" for Mao himself—the last stand of a great revolutionary against internal and external forces pressing him along that treacherous path from hero to despot. It was similarly the last stand of a collective expression of early revolutionary glory that he had epitomized. And it was perceived on several symbolic levels as a last stand against death itself—of the leader, of the revolution, and the individual in general.

On the Persistence of Thought Reform

Chinese thought reform has never disappeared. It was most intense, and most ambitious, during the period of my early work in the 1950s. At that time it took the form of a national spiritual cleansing, of a vast evangelical movement that combined steely coercion with visionary idealism. Over time thought reform has become less a source of conversion and inner purification than an expression of punishment. As I write this in early 2019, thought reform still presents itself as a means of bringing about general change but in actuality has become increasingly brutal in its application to those the regime views as its opponents or enemies.

An important turning point for thought reform has been the Chinese suppression of Falun Gong. Falun Gong emerged from the late twentieth-century boom in Qigong, an ancient Chinese practice consisting of meditation, slow-moving exercises, and regulated breathing. It was at first looked favorably upon by Chinese Communist leadership. But as Falun Gong's founder, Li Hongzhi, began to organize its estimated seventy million members, government authorities began to criticize the group sharply and interfere with its activities. Falun Gong then made what one writer called "perhaps the most ill-judged move in the history of peaceful protests," when, in 1999, ten thousand of its practitioners gathered near the government compound in Beijing to demand an end to official harassment, along with state recognition as a legal entity. But the regime viewed that demonstration as a challenge to the Party's uncontested ownership of both political reality and the nation itself, and responded with fierce condemnation of Falun Gong, widespread arrests, and versions of thought reform that included torture and notorious "reform through labor." (The government was acting partly out of anxious, still fresh memories of the Tiananmen Square uprising of 1989, when nearly a million Chinese protesters, mostly students, demanded greater democracy; Chinese troops attacked the protesters and killed perhaps three thousand of them and arrested as many as ten thousand.) There is also good evidence that considerable numbers of Falun Gong practitioners have been killed in order to provide organs for transplants, continuing a policy applied to other Chinese prisoners. And the government has required pledged denunciations of Falun Gong from faculty members, staff, and students of school and universities throughout China.

Of special interest here is the regime's justifications of its actions by declaring Falun Gong to be an "evil cult" that subjected its members to a "systematic form of mind control." The matter was complicated by a number of opinions voiced by American authorities on cults that Falun Gong was indeed a cult, that its members were robot-like in reflecting the words of its leader Li Hongzhi, and that Li himself had written and spoken about a vast apocalypse that he and Falun Gong members would survive, and of extraterrestrial beings who were somehow involved in the process. (Those claims by Li are usually left out of English translations of his writings.)

I had a small experience, or non-experience, in connection with that dispute when, after giving a talk at a meeting on cults and cultic behavior, I received an odd letter from a Chinese government official asking whether I would like to come to China to give talks on the behavior of cults. Clearly, the Chinese had Falun Gong in mind so I politely declined the invitation. My view is that the Chinese thought reform–related brutality is a human rights violation of a high order, even if the victims are part of a group that has cultist tendencies of its own. Of course these tendencies should be recognized, and there can be a situation of back-and-forth stimulation of totalistic groups, but that in no way exculpates the Chinese government for its brutal actions in its quest for the ownership of reality.

The Chinese government demonstrated a particularly flagrant form of cultist totalism in a series of 2017 show trials of human rights lawyers and activists. After facing various mixtures of psychological pressure and physical torture, the defendants made public confessions in which they accused themselves of seeking to "overthrow the socialist system," and expressed ostensible remorse for these harmful actions. These were reminders of Soviet show trials in the service of suppressing even the most modest forms of dissent, revealing the regime's anxiety about its difficulty in imposing its version of reality on its people.

But the most stunning revival of thought reform could be said to be that applied to members of the Uighur Muslim minority, which is the fifth most populous Chinese ethnic group and numbers as many as fifteen million people. The regime, since its beginnings, has had difficulty with the Uighurs, many of whom do not consider themselves Chinese and are active in separatist movements. Some have also joined jihadist groups and have become involved in violent incidents.

Since 2016, about a million Uighurs have been incarcerated in re-education camps with extensive electronic surveillance and subjected to varieties of thought reform that include forced violations of Muslim religion. "Re-education" has included pressure on Uighurs to eat pork and drink alcohol, and forcing men to shave their beards and women to remove their veils.

The reformers made use of isolation and torture for the extraction of confessions on how the Communist Party had "liberated" Muslims from religion and slavery. Uighurs have also been subjected to versions of "reform through labor" that, along with the extreme subjugation, made them unwilling contributors to the Chinese economy. The regime's cultural suppression of Uighurs has been compared to that of Tibetans, and the scope of this pervasive "re-education" has been compared to that of the Cultural Revolution. In one statement, a scholar even invoked the Nazis: "Cultural cleansing is Beijing's attempt to find a final solution to the Xinjiang [the home region of most Uighurs] problem." Thought reform's application to the Uighurs has been its most extreme effort at what might be called deculturalization.

There is another level to the dynamic. China is, among other things, a dictatorship. And Xi Jinping is an authoritarian dictator who has manipulated the rules of succession in order to remain in office, probably for life. He has been the most dictatorial leader since Mao, and his guruist identification with Mao is expressed in his having inserted into the Chinese constitution "The Thought of Xi Jinping." Moreover, his ascension to power has been accompanied by a certain amount of rehabilitation of the "cult of Mao" about a half century after the debacle of the Cultural Revolution. Xi has particularly emphasized the Maoist principle of "self-reliance," which can speak not only to individual but national behavior, and do so in a way that intensifies his claim to Mao-like greatness of his own.

Like Mao, Xi is fond of quoting Confucius and other classical Chinese figures, in keeping with a nationalistic resurgence. He has tightened control over all institutions, and has advocated draconian measures against any form of political resistance (although his "Thought" emphasizes harmony). One of his major projects has been a campaign against corruption, which enables him to attack actual or potential enemies even as he claims to be an agent of social purification. Thought reform is an ever-available method of purification in the service of dictatorship and authoritarian rule.

3

Ideological Totalism—
the "Eight Deadly Sins"

In my work I tend to look for possible generalizations that apply beyond immediate findings. Chapter 22 of my book on thought reform does that in connection with what I came to call the "eight deadly sins" of ideological totalism. When I wrote about them I knew that the themes were in no way confined to thought reform, and I spoke of them as taking us to a larger terrain that I called the "psychology of human zealotry."

But it is one thing to make such theoretical generalizations and quite another to have them viscerally confirmed by people who had experienced them in the very different setting of American cults. Because of that important connection, I have retained the entire chapter for this excerpt.

I came to realize that having a critical grasp of cultist behavior is an important step toward undermining claims of owned reality, and that this was best done from observations on actual human behavior. In that way the "eight deadly sins" became a kind of personal credo, both conceptual and ethical—a statement on where I stood on these elements of totalism and cultism.

Ideological Totalism
First published in 1961

Chinese Communist thought reform has a psychological momentum of its own, a self-perpetuating energy not always bound by the interests of the program's directors. When we inquire into the sources of this momentum, we come upon a complex set of psychological themes, which may be grouped under the general heading of *ideological totalism.* By this ungainly phrase I mean to suggest the coming together of immoderate ideology with equally immoderate individual character traits—an extremist meeting ground between people and ideas.

In discussing tendencies toward individual totalism within my subjects, I made it clear that these were a matter of degree, and that some potential for this form of all-or-nothing emotional alignment exists within everyone. Similarly, any ideology—that is, any set of emotionally charged convictions about humankind and its relationship to the natural or supernatural world—may be carried by its adherents in a totalistic direction. But this is most likely to occur with those ideologies that are most sweeping in their content and most ambitious—or messianic—in their claims, whether religious, political, or scientific. And where totalism exists, a religion, a political movement, or even a scientific organization becomes little more than an exclusive cult.

A discussion of what is most central in the thought reform environment can thus lead us to a more general consideration of the psychology of human zealotry. For in identifying, on the basis of this study of thought reform, features common to all expressions of ideological totalism, I wish to suggest a set of criteria against which any environment may be judged—a basis for answering the ever-recurring question: "Isn't this just like 'brainwashing'?"

These criteria consist of eight psychological themes that are predominant within the social field of the thought reform milieu. Each has a totalistic quality; each depends upon an equally absolute philosophical assumption; and each mobilizes certain individual emotional tendencies, mostly of a polarizing nature. Psychological theme, philosophical rationale, and polarized individual tendencies are interdependent; they require, rather than directly cause, each other. In combination they create an atmosphere that may temporarily energize or exhilarate, but that at the same time poses the gravest of human threats.

Milieu Control

The most basic feature of the thought reform environment, the psychological current upon which all else depends, is the control of human communication. Through this milieu control the totalist environment seeks to establish domain over not only the individual's communication with the outside (all that he or she sees and hears, reads and writes, experiences, and expresses), but also—in its penetration of one's inner life—over what we may speak of as one's communication with oneself. It creates an atmosphere uncomfortably reminiscent of George Orwell's *Nineteen Eighty-Four*—but with one important difference. Orwell, as a Westerner, envisioned milieu control accomplished by a mechanical device, the two-way "tele-screen." The Chinese, although they utilize whatever technical means they have at their disposal, achieve control of greater psychological depth through a *human* recording and transmitting apparatus: it is probably fair to say that the Chinese Communist prison and revolutionary university produce about as thoroughly controlled a group environment as has ever existed. The milieu control exerted over the broader social environment of Communist China, while considerably less intense, is in its own way unrivaled in its combination of extensiveness and depth; it is, in fact, one of the distinguishing features of Chinese Communist practice.

Such milieu control never succeeds in becoming absolute; and its own human apparatus can—when permeated by outside information—become subject to discordant "noise" beyond that of any mechanical apparatus. To totalist administrators, however, such occurrences are no more than evidences of "incorrect" use of the apparatus. For they look upon milieu control as a just and necessary policy, one which need not be kept secret: thought reform participants may be in doubt as to who is telling what to whom, but the fact that extensive information about everyone is being conveyed to the authorities is always known. At the center of this self-justification is their assumption of omniscience, their conviction that reality is their exclusive possession. Having experienced the impact of what they consider to be an ultimate truth (and having the need to dispel any possible inner doubts of their own), they consider it their duty to create an environment containing no more and no less than this "truth." In order to be the engineers of the human soul, they must first bring it under full observational control.

Many things happen psychologically to one exposed to milieu control; the most basic is the disruption of balance between self and outside world. Pressured toward a merger of internal and external milieus, individuals encounter a profound threat to personal autonomy. They are deprived of the combination of external information and inner reflection required to test the realities of their environment and to maintain a measure of identity separate from it. Instead, they are called upon to make an absolute polarization of the real (the prevailing ideology) and the unreal (everything else). To the extent that they do this, they undergo a *personal closure* that frees them from humanity's incessant struggle with the elusive subtleties of truth. They may even share their environment's sense of omniscience and assume a "God's-eye view" of the universe; but they are likely instead to feel victimized by the God's-eye view of the environment's controllers. At this point they are subject to the "hostility of suffocation," of which we have already spoken—the resentful awareness that their strivings toward new information, independent judgment, and self-expression are being thwarted. If their intelligence and sensibilities carry them toward realities outside the closed ideological system, they may resist these as not fully legitimate—until the milieu control is sufficiently diminished for them to share these realities with others. They are in either case profoundly hampered in the perpetual human quest for what is true, good, and relevant in the outside and within themselves.

Mystical Manipulation

The inevitable next step after milieu control is extensive personal manipulation. This manipulation assumes a no-holds-barred character, and uses every possible device at the milieu's command, no matter how bizarre or painful. Initiated from above, it seeks to provoke specific patterns of behavior and emotion in such a way that these will appear to have arisen spontaneously from within the environment. This element of planned spontaneity, directed as it is by an ostensibly omniscient group, must assume, for the manipulated, a near-mystical quality.

Ideological totalists do not pursue this approach *solely* for the purpose of maintaining a sense of power over others. Rather, they are impelled by a special kind of mystique that not only justifies such manipulations, but makes them mandatory. Included in this mystique is a sense of "higher purpose," of having "directly perceived some imminent law of social development," and of being themselves the vanguard of this development. By thus becoming the instruments of their own mystique, they create a mystical aura around the manipulating institutions—the Party, the Government, the Organization. They are the agents "chosen" (by history, by God, or by some other supernatural force) to carry out the "mystical imperative," the pursuit of which must supersede all considerations of decency or of immediate human welfare. Similarly, any thought or action that questions the higher purpose is considered to be stimulated by a lower purpose, to be backward, selfish, and petty in the face of the great, over-riding mission. This same mystical imperative produces the apparent extremes of idealism and cynicism that occur in connection with the manipulations of any totalist environment: even those actions that seem cynical in the extreme can be seen as having ultimate relationship to the "higher purpose."

At the level of the individual person, the psychological responses to this manipulative approach revolve around the basic polarity of trust and mistrust. One is asked to accept these manipulations on a basis of ultimate trust (or faith): "like a child in the arms of its mother," as one formerly imprisoned Westerner I interviewed in Hong Kong accurately perceived. One who trusts to this degree can accept the manipulations encountered, and may welcome their mysteriousness, find pleasure in their pain, and feel them to be necessary for the fulfillment of the "higher purpose" put forward. But such elemental trust is difficult to maintain; and even the strongest can be dissipated by constant manipulation.

When trust gives way to mistrust (or when trust has never existed), the higher purpose cannot serve as adequate emotional sustenance. The individual then responds to the manipulations through developing what I shall call the *psychology of the pawn*. Feeling unable to escape from forces more powerful than any individual, one subordinates everything to adapting to them. One becomes sensitive to all kinds of cues, expert at anticipating environmental pressures, and skillful in riding them in such a way that one's psychological energies merge with the tide rather than being turned painfully against oneself. This requires that one participate actively in the manipulation of others, as well as in the endless round of betrayals and self-betrayals that are required.

But whatever one's response—whether cheerful in the face of being manipulated, deeply resentful, or feeling a combination of both—one has been deprived of the opportunity to exercise one's capacities for self-expression and independent action.

The Demand for Purity

In the thought reform milieu, as in all situations of ideological totalism, the experiential world is sharply divided into the pure and the impure, into the absolutely good and the absolutely evil. The good and the pure are of course those ideas, feelings, and actions consistent with the totalist ideology and policy; anything else is apt to be relegated to the bad and the impure. Nothing human is immune from the flood of stern moral judgments. All "taints" and "poisons" that contribute to the existing state of impurity must be searched out and eliminated.

The philosophical assumption underlying this demand is that absolute purity (the "good Communist" or the ideal Communist state) is attainable, and that anything done to anyone in the name of this purity is ultimately moral. In actual practice, however, no one (and no political state) is really expected to achieve such perfection. Nor can this paradox be dismissed as merely a means of establishing a high standard to which all can aspire. Thought reform bears witness to its more malignant consequences: for by defining and manipulating the criteria of purity, and then by conducting an all-out war upon impurity, the ideological totalists create a narrow world of guilt and shame. This is perpetuated by an ethos of continuous reform, a demand that one strive permanently and painfully for something that not only does not exist but is in fact alien to the human condition.

At the level of the relationship between individual and environment, the demand for purity creates what we may term a *guilty milieu* and a *shaming milieu*. Since one's impurities are deemed sinful and potentially harmful to oneself and to others, one is, so to speak, expected to expect punishment—which results in a relationship of guilt with the environment. Similarly, when one fails to meet the prevailing standards in casting out such impurities, one is expected to expect humiliation and ostracism—thus establishing a relationship of shame. Moreover, the sense of guilt and the sense of shame become highly valued; they are preferred forms of communication, objects of public competition, and the bases for eventual bonds between the individual and his or her totalist accusers. One may attempt to simulate them for a while, but the subterfuge is likely to be detected, and it is safer to experience them genuinely.

People vary greatly in their susceptibilities to guilt and shame, depending upon patterns developed early in life. But since guilt and shame are basic to human existence, this variation can be no more than a matter of degree. All are made vulnerable through profound inner sensitivities to their own limitations and unfulfilled potential—that is, through their existential guilt. That existential guilt is available to totalistic manipulators who become the ultimate judges of good and evil. Universal tendencies toward guilt and shame become emotional levers for control and manipulation. The reformers become authorities without limit in dealing with others' limitations. And their power is nowhere more evident than in their capacity to "forgive."

One thus comes to apply the same totalist polarization of good and evil to judgments of one's own character: one tends to imbue certain aspects of oneself with excessive virtue, and even more excessively condemn other personal qualities—all according to their ideological standing. One must also look upon those impurities as originating from outside influences—that is, from the ever-threatening world beyond the closed, totalist ken. Therefore, one may seek to relieve oneself of some of one's burden of guilt by denouncing, continuously and hostilely, these same outside influences. The more guilty one feels, the greater the hatred, and the more threatening the outside influences seem. In this manner, the universal psychological tendency toward projection is nourished and institutionalized, leading to mass hatreds, purges of heretics, and political and religious holy wars. Moreover, the experience of totalist polarization of good and evil makes it very difficult to regain a more balanced inner sensitivity to the complexities of human morality. For there is no emotional bondage greater than that of the man or woman whose entire guilt potential—neurotic and existential—has become the property of ideological totalists.

The Cult of Confession

Closely related to the demand for absolute purity is an obsession with personal confession. Confession is carried beyond its ordinary religious, legal, and therapeutic expressions to the point of becoming a cult in itself. There is the demand that one confess to crimes one has not committed, to sinfulness that is artificially induced, in the name of a cure that is arbitrarily imposed. Such demands are made possible not only by the ubiquitous human tendencies toward guilt and shame but also by the need to give expression to these tendencies. In totalist hands, confession becomes a means of exploiting, rather than offering solace for, these vulnerabilities.

The totalist confession takes on a number of special meanings. It is first a vehicle for the kind of personal purification that we have just discussed, a means of maintaining a perpetual inner emptying or psychological purge of impurity; this *purging milieu* enhances the totalists' hold upon existential guilt. Second, it is an act of symbolic self-surrender, the expression of the merging of individual and environment. Third, it is a means of maintaining an ethos of total exposure—a policy of making public (or at least known to the Organization) everything possible about the life experiences, thoughts, and passions of each individual, and especially those elements that might be regarded as derogatory.

The assumption underlying total exposure is the environment's claim to total ownership of each individual self within it. Private ownership of the mind and its products—of imagination or of memory—becomes highly immoral. The accompanying rationale (or rationalization) is familiar to us; the milieu has attained such a perfect state of enlightenment that any individual retention of ideas or emotions has become anachronistic.

The cult of confession can offer the individual person meaningful psychological satisfactions in the continuing opportunity for emotional catharsis and for relief of suppressed guilt feelings, especially insofar as these are associated with self-punitive tendencies to get pleasure from personal degradation. More than this, the sharing of confession and enthusiasm can create an orgiastic sense of "oneness," of the most intense intimacy with fellow confessors and of the dissolution of self into the great flow of the Movement. And there is also, at least initially, the possibility of genuine self-revelation and of self-betterment through the recognition that "the thing that has been exposed is what I am."

But as totalist pressures turn confession into recurrent command performances, the element of histrionic public display takes precedence over genuine inner experience. One becomes concerned with the effectiveness of personal performance, and this performance sometimes comes to serve the function of evading the very emotions and ideas about which one feels most guilty—confirming the statement by one of Camus's characters that "authors of confessions write especially to avoid confessing, to tell nothing of what they know."

The difficulty, of course, lies in the inevitable confusion that takes place between the actor's method and separate personal reality, between the performer and the "real me."

In this sense, the cult of confession has effects quite the reverse of its ideal of total exposure: rather than eliminating personal secrets, it increases and intensifies them. In any situation the personal secret has two important elements: first, guilty and shameful ideas that one wishes to suppress in order to prevent their becoming known by others or their becoming too prominent in one's own awareness; and second, representations of parts of oneself too precious to be expressed except when alone or when involved in special loving relationships formed around this shared secret world. Personal secrets are always maintained in opposition to inner pressures toward self-exposure. The totalist milieu makes contact with these inner pressures through its own obsession with the unmasking process. As a result, old secrets are revived and new ones proliferate; the latter frequently consist of resentments toward or doubts about the Movement, or else are related to aspects of identity still existing outside of the prescribed ideological sphere. Each person becomes caught up in a continuous conflict over which secrets to preserve and which to surrender, over ways to reveal lesser secrets in order to protect more important ones; over boundaries between the secret and the known, between the public and the private. And around one secret, or a complex of secrets, there may revolve an ultimate inner struggle between resistance and self-surrender.

Finally, the cult of confession makes it virtually impossible to attain a reasonable balance between worth and humility. The enthusiastic and aggressive confessor becomes like Camus's character whose perpetual confession is his means of judging others: "[I] . . . practice the profession of penitent to be able to end up as a judge . . . the more I accuse myself, the more I have a right to judge you." The identity of the "judge-penitent" thus becomes a vehicle for taking on some of the environment's arrogance and sense of omnipotence. Yet even this shared omnipotence cannot protect one from the opposite (but not unrelated) feelings of humiliation and weakness, feelings especially prevalent among those who remain more the enforced penitent than the all-powerful judge.

The "Sacred Science"

The totalist milieu maintains an aura of sacredness around its basic dogma, holding it out as an ultimate moral vision for the ordering of human existence. This sacredness is evident in the prohibition (whether or not explicit) against the questioning of basic assumptions, and in the reverence that is demanded for the originators of the Word, the present bearers of the Word, and the Word itself. While thus transcending ordinary concerns of logic, however, the milieu at the same time makes an exaggerated claim of airtight logic, of absolute "scientific" precision. Thus the ultimate moral vision becomes an ultimate science; and the person who dares to criticize it, or to harbor even unspoken alternative ideas, becomes not only immoral and irreverent, but also "unscientific." In this way, the philosopher-kings of modern ideological totalism reinforce their authority by claiming to share in the rich and respected heritage of natural science.

The assumption here is not so much that humans can be God, but rather that our *ideas* can be God: that an absolute science of ideas (and implicitly, an absolute science of humankind) exists, or is at least very close to being attained; that this science can be combined with an equally absolute body of moral principles; and that the resulting doctrine is true for all people at all times. Although no ideology goes quite this far in overt statement, such assumptions are implicit in totalist practice.

At the level of the individual, the totalist sacred science can offer much comfort and security. Its appeal lies in its seeming unification of the mystical and the logical modes of experience (in psychoanalytic terms, of the *primary* and *secondary* thought processes). For within the framework of the sacred science, there is room for both careful step-by-step syllogism and sweeping, nonrational "insights." Since the distinction between the logical and the mystical is, to begin with, artificial and man-made, an opportunity for transcending it can create an extremely intense feeling of truth. But the posture of unquestioning faith—both rationally and nonrationally derived—is not easy to sustain, especially if one discovers that the world of experience is not nearly as absolute as the sacred science claims it to be.

Yet so strong a hold can the sacred science achieve over one's mental processes that if one begins to feel attracted to ideas that either contradict or ignore it, one may become guilty and afraid. One's quest for knowledge is consequently hampered, since in the name of science one is prevented from engaging in the receptive search for truth that characterizes the genuinely scientific approach. And one's position is made more difficult by the absence, in a totalist environment, of any distinction between the sacred and the profane: there is no thought or action that cannot be related to the sacred science. To be sure, one can usually find areas of experience outside its immediate authority; but during periods of maximum totalist activity (like thought reform) any such areas are cut off, and there is virtually no escape from the milieu's ever-pressing edicts and demands. Whatever combination of continued adherence, inner resistance, or compromise between them the individual person adopts toward this blend of counterfeit science and backdoor religion, it represents another continuous pressure toward personal closure, toward avoiding, rather than grappling with, the kinds of knowledge and experience necessary for genuine self-expression and creative development.

Loading the Language

The language of the totalist environment is characterized by the thought-terminating cliché. The most far-reaching and complex of human problems are compressed into brief, highly reductive, definitive-sounding phrases, easily memorized and easily expressed. These become the start and finish of any ideological analysis. In thought reform, for instance, the phrase "bourgeois mentality" is used to encompass and critically dismiss ordinarily troublesome concerns like the quest for individual expression, the exploration of alternative ideas, and the search for perspective and balance in political judgments. And in addition to their function as interpretive shortcuts, these clichés become what Richard Weaver has called "ultimate terms": either "god terms," representative of ultimate good; or "devil terms," representative of ultimate evil. In thought reform, "progress," "progressive," "liberation," "proletarian standpoints" and "the dialectic of history" fall into the former category; "capitalist," "imperialist," "exploiting classes," and "bourgeois" (mentality/liberalism/morality/superstition/greed) of course fall into the latter. Totalist language, then, is repetitiously centered on all-encompassing jargon, prematurely abstract, highly categorical, relentlessly judging, and to anyone but its most devoted advocate, deadly dull: in Lionel Trilling's phrase, "the language of nonthought."

To be sure, this kind of language exists to some degree within any cultural or organizational group, and all systems of belief depend upon it. It is in part an expression of unity and exclusiveness: as Edward Sapir put it, " 'He talks like us' is equivalent to saying 'He is one of us.' " The loading of language is much more extreme in ideological totalism, however, since the jargon expresses the claimed certitudes of the sacred science. Also involved is an underlying assumption that language—like all other human products—can be owned and operated by the Movement. No compunctions are felt about manipulating or loading it in any fashion; the only consideration is its usefulness to the cause.

For an individual person, the effect of the language of ideological totalism can be summed up in one word: constriction.

One is, so to speak, linguistically deprived; and since language is so central to all human experience, one's capacities for thinking and feeling are immensely narrowed. This is what one of my Chinese subjects meant when he said, "Using the same pattern of words for so long . . . you feel chained." Actually, not everyone exposed *feels* chained, but in effect everyone is profoundly confined by these verbal fetters. As in other aspects of totalism, this loading of language may provide an initial sense of insight and security, which is eventually followed by uneasiness. This uneasiness may result in a retreat into a rigid orthodoxy in which an individual shouts the ideological jargon all the louder in order to demonstrate conformity, hide conflict and despair, and ward off the fear and guilt that would result from using words and phrases other than the correct ones. Or else one may experience a complex pattern of inner division, and dutifully produce the expected clichés in public performances while in private moments searching for more meaningful avenues of expression. Either way, imagination becomes increasingly dissociated from actual life experiences and may even tend to atrophy from disuse.

Doctrine over Person

This sterile language reflects another characteristic feature of ideological totalism: the subordination of human experience to the claims of doctrine. This primacy of doctrine over person is evident in the continual shift between experience itself and the highly abstract interpretation of such experience—between genuine feelings and spurious cataloging of feelings. It has much to do with the peculiar aura of half-reality that a totalist environment seems, at least to the outsider, to possess.

John K. Fairbank and Mary C. Wright described this tendency in the totalist approach of Chinese Communism to broad historical events:

> Stock characters like capitalist imperialists from abroad, feudal and semi-feudal reaction at home, and the resistance and liberation movements of "the people" enact a morality play. This melodrama sees aggression, injustice, exploitation, and humiliation engulf the Chinese people until salvation comes at last with Communism. Mass revolutions require an historical myth as part of their black and white morality, and this is the ideological myth of one of the great revolutions of world history.

The inspiriting force of such myths cannot be denied; nor can one ignore their capacity for mischief. For when the myth becomes fused with the totalist sacred science, the resulting "logic" can be so compelling and coercive that it simply replaces the realities of individual experience. Consequently, past historical events are retrospectively altered, wholly rewritten, or ignored, to make them consistent with the doctrinal logic. This alteration becomes especially malignant when its distortions are imposed upon individual memory, as occurred in the false confessions extracted during thought reform in China.

The same doctrinal primacy prevails in the totalist approach to changing people: the demand that character and identity be reshaped, not in accordance with one's special nature or potentialities, but rather to fit the rigid contours of the doctrinal mold. The human is thus subjugated to the ahuman. And in this manner, the totalists, as Camus phrases it, "put an abstract idea above human life, even if they call it history, to which they themselves have submitted in advance and to which they will decide quite arbitrarily, to submit everyone else as well."

The underlying assumption is that the doctrine—including its mythological elements—is ultimately more valid, true, and real than is any aspect of actual human character or human experience. Thus, even when circumstances require that a totalist movement follow a course of action in conflict with or outside of the doctrine, there exists what Benjamin Schwartz has described as a "will to orthodoxy," which requires an elaborate facade of new rationalizations designed to demonstrate the unerring consistency of the doctrine and the unfailing foresight it provides. The greater importance of this will to orthodoxy lies in more hidden manifestations, particularly the totalists' pattern of imposing their doctrine-dominated remolding upon people in order to seek confirmation of (and again, dispel their own doubts about) this same doctrine. Rather than modify the myth in accordance with experience, the will to orthodoxy requires instead that men be modified in order to reaffirm the myth. Thus, much of prison thought reform was devoted to making Westerners conform to the pure image of "evil imperialist," so that they could take their proper roles in the Communist morality play of Chinese history.

The individual person under such doctrine-dominated pressure to change is thrust into an intense struggle with integrity, a struggle that takes place in relation to polarized feelings of "sincerity" and "insincerity." In a totalist environment, absolute "sincerity" is demanded; and the major criterion for sincerity is likely to be one's degree of doctrinal compliance—both in regard to belief and to direction of personal change. Yet there is always the possibility of retaining an alternative version of sincerity (and of reality), the capacity to imagine a different kind of existence and another form of sincere commitment (as did another of my Chinese subjects when she thought, "The world could not be like this"). These alternative visions depend upon such things as the strength of previous identity, the penetration of the milieu by outside ideas, and the retained capacity for eventual individual renewal. The totalist environment, however, counters such "deviant" tendencies with the accusation that they stem entirely from personal "problems" ("thought problems" or "ideological problems") derived from untoward earlier ("bourgeois") influences. The outcome will depend largely upon how much genuine relevance the doctrine has for the individual emotional predicament. And even for those to whom it seems totally appealing, the exuberant sense of well-being it temporarily affords may be more a "delusion of wholeness" than an expression of true and lasting inner harmony.

The Dispensing of Existence

The totalist environment draws a sharp line between those whose right to existence can be recognized, and those who possess no such right. In thought reform, as in Chinese Communist practice generally, the world is divided into the "people" (defined as "the working class, the peasant class, the petite bourgeoisie, and the national bourgeoisie"), and the "reactionaries" or "lackeys of imperialism" (defined as "the landlord class, the bureaucratic capitalist class, and the Kuomintang reactionaries and their henchmen"). Mao Zedong makes the existential distinction between the two groups quite explicit:

> Under the leadership of the working class and the Communist Party, these classes [the people] unite together to form their own state and elect their own government [so as to] carry out a dictatorship over the lackeys of imperialism. . . . These two aspects, namely, democracy among the people and dictatorship over the reactionaries, combine to form the people's democratic dictatorship. . . . To the hostile classes the state apparatus is the instrument of oppression. It is violent, and not "benevolent." . . . Our benevolence applies only to the people, and not to the reactionary acts of the reactionaries and reactionary classes outside the people.

Being "outside the people," the reactionaries are presumably nonpeople. Under conditions of ideological totalism, in China and elsewhere, nonpeople have often been put to death, their executioners then becoming guilty (in Camus's phrase) of "crimes of logic." But the thought reform process is one means by which nonpeople are permitted, through a change in attitude and personal character, to make themselves over into people. The most literal example of such dispensing of existence and nonexistence is to be found in the sentence given to certain political criminals: execution in two years' time, unless during that two-year period they have demonstrated genuine progress in their reform.

The dispensing of human existence is a flagrant expression of what the Greeks called *hubris*, of arrogant humans claiming to be God. Yet one underlying assumption makes this arrogance mandatory: the conviction that there is just one path to true existence, just one valid mode of being, and that all others are perforce invalid and false. Totalists thus feel themselves compelled to destroy all possibilities of false existence as a means of furthering the great plan of true existence to which they are committed. Indeed, Mao's words suggest that all of thought reform can be viewed as a way to eradicate such allegedly false modes of existence—not only among the nonpeople, within whom these modes supposedly originate, but also among legitimate people allegedly contaminated by them.

> The [function of the] people's state is to protect the people. Only where there is the people's state, is it possible for the people to use democratic methods on a nationwide and all-round scale to educate and reform

themselves, to free themselves from the influence of reactionaries at home and abroad . . . to unlearn the bad habits and ideas acquired from the old society and not to let themselves travel on the erroneous path pointed out by the reactionaries, but to continue to advance and develop towards a Socialist and Communist society accomplishing the historic mission of completely eliminating classes and advancing towards a universal fraternity.

Experiencing the polar emotional conflict of "being versus nothingness," the individual is likely to be drawn to a conversion experience, which he or she sees as the only means of attaining a path of existence for the future. The totalist environment—even when it does not resort to physical abuse—thus stimulates in everyone a fear of extinction or annihilation much like the basic fear experienced by Western prisoners. A person can overcome this fear and find (in Martin Buber's term) "confirmation," not in individual relationships, but only from the fount of all existence, the totalist Organization. Existence comes to depend upon creed ("I believe, therefore I am"), upon submission ("I obey, therefore I am") and beyond these, upon a sense of total merger with the ideological movement. Ultimately, of course, one compromises and combines the totalist "confirmation" with independent elements of personal identity; but is ever made aware that if one strays too far along this "erroneous path," one's right to existence may be withdrawn.

The more clearly an environment expresses these eight

psychological themes, the greater its resemblance to ideological totalism; and the more it utilizes such totalist devices to change people, the greater its resemblance to thought reform (or "brainwashing"). But facile comparisons can be misleading. No milieu ever achieves complete totalism, and many relatively moderate environments show some signs of it. Moreover, totalism tends to be recurrent rather than continuous: in China, for instance, its fullest expression occurs during thought reform; it is less apparent during lulls in thought reform, although it is by no means absent. And like the "enthusiasm" with which it is often associated, totalism is more apt to be present during the early phases of mass movements than later—in the 1950s Communist China was more totalist than Soviet Russia. But if totalism has at any time been prominent in a movement, there is always the possibility of its reappearance, even after long periods of relative moderation.

Some environments, then, also come perilously close to totalism but at the same time keep alternative paths open; this combination can offer unusual opportunities for achieving intellectual and emotional depth. And even the most full-blown totalist milieu can provide (more or less despite itself) a valuable and enlarging life experience—*if* the individual exposed has both the opportunity to leave the extreme environment and the inner capacity to absorb and make inner use of the totalist pressures.

In addition, ideological totalism itself may offer an intense peak experience: a sense of transcending all that is ordinary and prosaic, of being freed from the encumbrances of human ambivalence, of entering a sphere of truth, reality, trust, and sincerity beyond any previously known or even imagined. But these peak experiences, the result as they are of external pressure, distortion, and threat, carry a great potential for rebound, and for equally intense opposition to the very things that initially seem so liberating. Such imposed peak experiences—as contrasted with those more freely and privately arrived at by great religious leaders and mystics—are essentially experiences of personal closure. Rather than stimulating greater receptivity and "openness to the world," they encourage a backward step into some form of "embeddedness"—a retreat into doctrinal and organizational exclusiveness, and into all-or-nothing emotional patterns more characteristic (at least at this stage of human history) of the child than of the individuated adult.

And if no peak experience occurs, ideological totalism does even greater violence to the human potential: it evokes destructive emotions, produces intellectual and psychological constrictions, and deprives people of all that is most subtle and imaginative—under the false promise of eliminating those very imperfections and ambivalences that help to define the human condition. This combination of personal closure, self-destructiveness, and hostility toward outsiders leads to the dangerous group excesses so characteristic of ideological totalism in any form. It also mobilizes extremist tendencies in those outsiders under attack, thus creating a vicious circle of totalism.

What is the source of ideological totalism? How do these extremist emotional patterns originate? These questions raise the most crucial and the most difficult of human problems.

Behind ideological totalism lies the ever-present human quest for the omnipotent guide—for the supernatural force, political party, shared ideas, great leader, or precise science—that will bring ultimate solidarity to humankind and eliminate the terror of death and nothingness. This quest is evident in the mythologies, religions, and histories of all nations, as well as in every individual life. The degree to which an one embraces totalism depends greatly upon factors in one's personal history: early lack of trust, extreme environmental chaos, total domination by a parent or parent-representative, intolerable burdens of guilt, and severe crises of identity. Thus an early sense of confusion and dislocation, or an early experience of unusually intense family milieu control, can later produce a complete intolerance for confusion and dislocation, and a longing for the reinstatement of milieu control. But these things are in some measure part of every childhood experience; and therefore the potential for totalism is a continuum from which no one entirely escapes, and in relationship to which no two people are exactly the same.

It may be that the capacity for totalism is most fundamentally a product of human childhood itself, of the prolonged period of helplessness and dependency through which each of us must pass. Limited as they are, infants have no choice but to imbue their first nurturing authorities—their parents—with an exaggerated omnipotence, until the time they are themselves capable of some degree of independent action and judgment. And even as they develop into children and adolescents, they continue to require many of the all-or-none polarities of totalism as terms with which to define their intellectual, emotional, and moral worlds. Under favorable circumstances (that is, when family and culture encourage individuation) these requirements can be replaced by more flexible and moderate tendencies; but they never entirely disappear.

During adult life, individual totalism takes on new contours as it becomes associated with new ideological interests. It may become part of the configuration of personal emotions, messianic ideas, and organized mass movement that I have described as ideological totalism. When it does, we cannot speak of it as simply a form of regression. It is partly this, but it is also something more: a new form of adult embeddedness, originating in patterns of security-seeking carried over from childhood, but with qualities of ideas and aspirations that are specifically adult. During periods of cultural crisis and of rapid historical change, the totalist quest for the omnipotent guide leads men and women to seek to become that guide.

Totalism, then, is a widespread phenomenon, but it is not the only approach to re-education. We can best use our knowledge of it by applying its criteria to familiar processes in our own cultural tradition and in our own country.

4

On Cultism and the Larger Society

Once chapter 22 of my thought reform book was appropriated (in the late 1970s and early 1980s) by young people involved with cults, or by their parents, I was drawn into the national conversation. I began to receive two antithetical forms of pressure: first, from anti-cult groups (former members, parents, and social commentators) to denounce these groups carte blanche and especially their "brainwashing"; and from civil libertarians, to denounce the misuse of my work by "deprogrammers" who could apply their own coercive methods in forcibly kidnapping cult members and pointing out how their group resorts to the themes of ideological totalism I had described. My general position was to oppose coercion at either end, but the situation called for additional explanation.

The subject was much more excruciating than this essay may suggest—excruciating for parents who experienced their children's cult involvement as a painfully extreme rejection, for the young recruits themselves as they experienced the powerful conflicts mobilized by cults; and for American society in general in its commitment to freedom of religion on the one hand, and protection of its young people against harm and fraud on the other.

To understand the cultic contribution to the behavior of mental predators, it is useful to look briefly at the meanings associated with the word "cult" over the past few centuries. The English word cult, derived from the French *culte* and the Latin *coltus*, was first used in the early seventeenth century and referred to religious worship in general and homage to a divine being. An Oxford English Dictionary entry referring to 1613 usage speaks of "adoration . . . for a diuine cult, and worship." But over time, the word "cult" came to represent worship or veneration "directed towards a specific figure or object." And another entry referring to a 1679 usage distinguishes cults from genuine religion: "Let not every circumstantial difference or Variety of Cult be Nick-named a new Religion."

In a sense, "cult" became a modern word to describe ancient groups and deities. But by the early modem era (seventeenth century), distinctions came to be made between the relatively narrow cultic focus on specific individuals and objects, and more broadly gauged general religions. Hence the references to cults of particular gods or goddesses or sacred personages: of Dionysus and Aphrodite from the Greeks, and of Mary from later Catholic worship.

The ancient cults, religious scholars tell us, were integral to their societies as part of a flow of worship and organization that provided form and continuity. (The word cult is related to "culture" and "cultivate.") In contrast, contemporary cultist groups—not only extremist guru-led spiritual communities but Chinese thought-reformers as well—go against the grain of their immediate or recent societies. Indeed they seek to replace those societies with something close to the absolutism of premodern cults.

In that way contemporary cultist behavior is a form of restorationism, of recreating versions of idealized past communities. Cultist movements can be idiosyncratic in combining bits and pieces of ancient teachings. Aum Shinrikyō, for instance, brought together Buddhist, Hindu, and Christian principles as interwoven in the mind of the guru. Or these movements may attack ancient principles even as they make use of those principles, as in the case of the Chinese Communists' attack on Confucianism while employing the Confucian principles of "rectification" and "re-education."

But to impose those ancient principles on contemporary minds, cultic groups must remove from those minds the long-standing psychological and political effects of modern multiplicity and pluralism. That cannot be done without reverting to extreme measures that include intense psychological and physical assaults to extract confessions and sustain fierce expressions of mutual criticism and self-criticism. The project becomes sacred, imbued with what cultic enforcers can experience as a "higher purpose" that justifies the most draconian measures.

There is a Sisyphean element in all this: the cultist purifiers cannot roll their ideological rock to the top of the hill of reality control. They can impose their reality on many for a considerable period of time, but they ultimately discover that the human mind is not completely manipulable, that sooner or later they will encounter what I speak of as the hostility of suffocation and the law of diminishing conversions.

To be sure, cultist groups can do enormous harm while pursuing their sacred mission, yet these doubts are bound to occur. One response to such doubts can be a plunge ever more deeply into the sacred mission. But this tension between cultist mission and emerging doubt may never quite go away.

No wonder that the term "cult" has become pejorative. That was so in the seventeenth-century warning against the narrow cultic focus and holds true today. Of course, attacks on groups deemed cultic by established religions, then and now, have elements of struggles over spiritual turf. But also at issue is the tendency of cultic groups to create a narrow, coercive reality centered on the urgent apocalyptic impulses of a deified leader.

It is hard to know just when such cults turn violent, whether toward members who question its imposed reality or seek to leave, or toward the larger world in connection with the cult's intense apocalyptic impulses.

Such large-scale violence erupted shockingly in November 1978 with more than nine hundred people found dead in a jungle clearing in Guyana, all members of a cult called Peoples Temple, which had retreated to that small nation on the northeastern coast of South America. The apocalyptic event triggered by Jim Jones, the guru of Peoples Temple, was a call to "revolutionary suicide," which was his particular apocalyptic ideology. But it turned out that more than half of those dead people had been murdered by other cult members carrying out Jones's insistence that everyone die.

At that time, I happened to be traveling in Germany interviewing Nazi doctors, and was struck not only by the enormity of the killing but by the agent used, cyanide (mixed in a Kool-Aid-like drink), all too reminiscent of the cyanide content of the Zyklon B used in Auschwitz gas chambers.

Peoples Temple and Aum Shinrikyō were very different cults. But in each case there was an unstable guru with considerable charisma and religious and organizational talent who moved in and out of psychosis and embraced violence as a form of immortalizing his cult and himself. With Aum Shinrikyō that immortalization took the form of apocalyptic activism, of "forcing the end." With Jim Jones, the apocalyptic activism was that of cultic self-destruction, of collective "revolutionary suicide" so pressing that something on the order of cult-wide coercive suicide had to be carried out, along with the simple killing of those who could not or would not kill themselves.

To be sure, such violence is not found in the great majority of cults. But there is a widespread dynamic of potential violence, having to do with a combination of worship of an unstable guru, thought reform–like procedures, and an inward turning of fiercely apocalyptic impulses. Yet, in a democracy, even potentially violent groups are not illegal. Their totalism and cultism can be abhorrent to many of us, but need not break any laws. Unless, that is, there is demonstrable harm done to members or outsiders, and equally demonstrable deception or fraud. It was under these two rubrics that cases were mounted against cultic groups, usually by parents of members.

When those cases against cults were mounted and legal decisions made against the cults, young members could manifest a surprising "deconversion" and reversion to something close to their pre-cult worldview and identity. This turnabout came to be called "snapping," and could sometimes occur soon after the young cult member sat down with his or her lawyer and parents in the court room. To be sure, there could remain considerable conflict, confusion, and anxiety, but the phenomenon suggests that a pre-cult constellation had remained within the self, however inactively, after the conversion to the cult worldview and after months or years of living in the cultist environment.

One could say that the original conversion involved the creation of a second functional self, or what I have called "doubling," without elimination of the pre-cult self. And that each "self" had a claim on consciousness and behavior that was much influenced by the pulls of the immediate environment. The phenomenon of snapping tells us that, whatever the intensity of the embrace of cultism, an alternative to it can be unexpectedly available. This suggests that cultlike behavior is affected by context, and by large social and historical issues, and cannot be completely "solved" by psychiatrists, theologians, or any other professional group.

The cultist penetration of American consciousness was both reflected and greatly increased by a 2018 Netflix television series about an Oregon-based cult in the 1980s, the

Rajneeshees, which was responsible for the first significant episode of bioterrorism on United States soil. A six-part series, it was remarkable for its nuanced presentation of the mindsets of both cultists and local people. Especially notable was a sequence of events in the series from the group's initial creative energies in building a small city to its resort to violence against its own members and its Oregon neighbors. The violence consisted of the mass salmonella poisoning of food served in various prominent restaurants, causing a number of deaths and infections in hundreds of people. The series depicted conflicts between cultists and local people, the exploitation of members' idealism by the cult's leaders, and the corruption of both guru (who accumulated ninety-three Rolls-Royces) and his chief disciple. The series also gave one the sense that the United States is great terrain for cults, with its enormous financial and other resources and its longstanding principle of "newness"—but also that America can be relentless in its opposition to threats from cultist groups that seem alien to much of its social norms.

Fascination with cultist behavior, in America and elsewhere, never quite goes away. That is because of the widespread attraction to cultist certainty and the fascination with the primal nature of the cultist drama.

In considering the sources of cultist totalism or fundamentalism, I want to stress the enormous significance of what I call historical or psychohistorical dislocation in contemporary life. Such dislocation derives from the weakening of the institutions that organize the life cycle and its belief systems—whether involving religion, authority, governance, marriage, family, or death. Many of these institutions, having lost their internal coherence, become burdensome. Cults can provide substitute structures that have intensity and meaning for many young (and not so young) people. When one talks about totalism or cultism, one can never step out of history.

Many cults are both radical and reactionary. They are radical in that they raise uncomfortable issues about middle-class family life and general values in American society: issues concerning hypocritical approaches to spirituality, liberalism, pluralism, materialism, and overall moral advocacy. In this sense, cults show some continuity with spiritual movements of the 1960s and early 1970s. The apparent radicalism can make them appealing to young people and accounts for part, although by no means all, of their elders' resistance to cults. But cults are reactionary in the sense of returning to premodern structures of authority, sometimes to the extent of establishing patterns of internal fascism in their organizational structure.

Imagery of extinction (related to nuclear weapons) is also very much a historical factor that influences patterns of fundamentalism throughout the world. The term "fundamentalism" derives from an early twentieth-century American Protestant movement that sought to stem the liberal theological tide and to restate what were considered to be the fundamental doctrines of the Christian faith. Intense embrace of those "fundamentals" could lapse into the biblical literalism of fundamentalism. Cults tend to express a communal fundamentalism.

They also provide a communal initiation rite in the transition to early adult life, the stage of the life cycle of many cult recruits. Such a rite offers ritual and symbolic structures not available in the larger culture and enables disciples to enter into their guru's immortalizing realm. Key to the initiation rite are "high" or transcendent states, which are described with great intensity by those who have experienced them. These high states can be particularly important in the working out of adolescent and young adult struggles, but can become suspect when an initiate faces doubt about a cult.

From my perspective, cults are primarily a social and historical issue. Of course they raise individual-psychological concerns of great importance, and there is a place for psychologists and psychiatrists in understanding cult members and treating them when they need it. But I believe that psychological professionals can best contribute in the area of education. There have certainly been repercussions from our increasing knowledge about cults; many cults have had difficulty obtaining members since their patterns of deception have become more recognizable and less effective.

Psychiatrists and theologians have in common the need for a certain modesty here. They need to avoid playing God and to reject the notion that we have anything like a complete solution. Of course there remain painful moral dilemmas. Where laws are violated—through fraud or specific harm done to recruits—legal intervention is clearly required. But what of situations of a kind I have seen in which young people involved in intense cult situations have become virtually automatized, their behavior rote, their language little but cliché, and yet express a certain satisfaction or even happiness in that state? We do well to continue to focus on our commitment to individual autonomy and to identify and combat patterns of violence.

Part Two

World-Ending Threats

5

Aum Shinrikyō

In combining ultimate fanaticism with ultimate weapons, Aum Shinrikyō (1984–95) was a new and highly dangerous manifestation of cultism. Like many other cults and political movements, Aum was apocalyptic. Its apocalypticism was not only fierce but activist. Aum's guru, Shōkō Asahara, impressed on his followers the responsibility of joining in the military struggle that would bring on Armageddon and provide a means for the surviving remnant to take the lead in creating a purified world. Aum created a cultic project of destroying the world.

That was of course the most grandiose of missions, and Aum did not end up making much of a contribution to it. But Aum's scientists did succeed in producing and releasing very crude versions of chemical and biological weapons and sought unsuccessfully to acquire nuclear weapons as well. In its embrace of weapons of mass destruction, Aum was translating its nuclearized apocalyptic vision into actual steps taken in the real world.

Given his world-ending proclivities, we should not be surprised that Asahara strongly admired two of the twentieth century's greatest annihilators of their fellow human beings, Adolf Hitler and Mao Zedong.

Significantly, Asahara was obsessed with Hiroshima and its suggestion of world destruction. In what he called his "meditations," he described his "astral body" separating from his physical body and arriving in a devastated Hiroshima populated by moribund survivors consumed by radiation effects. He alone could transcend these effects and render Hiroshima an important part of his world-ending story.

Apocalyptic activism has a very long history. According to Gershom Scholem, a leading authority on Jewish mysticism, the practice was known to ancient rabbis as "forcing the end." At issue was a moral question: given the inevitability of violence prior to the appearance of the messiah, should one join in that violence to hasten the messianic moment? The rabbis, in their wisdom, decided that "forcing the end" in that way would be an expression of undesirable "impatience" and that only God could set a messianic timetable. Aum Shinrikyō demonstrated that contemporary cultists need feel no such restraint.

Apocalyptic narratives are always about survival, and in this one only Asahara and his closest disciples would be among the surviving remnant. The nuclear holocaust in his view would be a form of karmic "cleansing," and he and his disciples would find food free of radioactive contamination. But on the matter of survival, there is another important point to note. Aum disciples had no standing other than their merging with the guru, absorbing him, becoming part of him, or in their own parlance, becoming "clones" of Asahara. And since only those whose merger with the guru was most complete would survive, the guru himself *would be the lone survivor, would be what has been described in the literature on paranoid grandiosity as "the last man to remain alive."*

To understand the reach of cultism, it is useful to briefly compare Aum Shinrikyō with ISIS in terms of our perceptions of the two groups. We think of Aum Shinrikyō primarily as a fanatical religious cult with a fierce measure of apocalypticism. We then learn that its apocalyptic engine, along with its totalistic claim to the dispensing of existence, propelled it into violent terrorist actions.

We view ISIS as primarily a terrorist group and an army, but we discover that it too has a powerful version of end time that, in its world destruction, eliminates both non-Islamic Westerners and Muslims with alternate views; it also contains a messianic restoration of the ancient Islamic caliphate, the state ruled by an authentic religious successor of the prophet Muhammad. In its aggressive militarism, ISIS too takes a stand of "forcing the end." This apocalyptic narrative has been weakened by ISIS' loss of the territory believed necessary for the renewal of the caliphate. But the narrative has never been renounced as ISIS continues to attract jihadist fighters from all over the Islamic world. For ISIS the apocalyptic narrative is still murderous.

Aum, in contrast, effectively was ended as a violent group by Japanese police action and imprisonment and execution of the guru. Japanese authorities were slow to carry out the death penalty on Asahara out of concern that he become viewed as a martyr, but in 2018 they eventually did hang him, together with six other leading members of Aum, after twenty-three years of imprisonment. While Aum no longer exists, the group has been partly reconstituted under the name Aleph, which renounces violence while otherwise continuing to embrace much of Asahara's thought.

One could say that with Aum and ISIS, the retained apocalyptic vision becomes a kind of anchor—by no means a source of stability but rather one of continuity and ever-available, frequently violent, energy. And for both, that vision includes a promise of perpetual cultic cleansing, together with the claim of ownership of death itself.

Aum Shinrikyō
First published in 1999

On March 20, 1995, Aum Shinrikyō, a fanatical Japanese religious cult, released sarin, a deadly nerve gas, on five subway trains during Tokyo's early-morning rush hour. A male cult member boarded each of the trains carrying two or three small plastic bags covered with newspaper and, at an agreed-upon time, removed the newspaper and punctured the bags with a sharpened umbrella tip. On the trains, in the stations where they stopped, and at the station exits, people coughed, choked, experienced convulsions, and collapsed. Eleven were killed and up to five thousand injured. Had Aum succeeded in producing a purer form of the gas, the deaths could have been in the thousands or hundreds of thousands, for sarin, produced originally by the Nazis, is among the most lethal of chemical weapons. Those releasing it on the trains understood themselves to be acting on behalf of their guru and his vast plan for human salvation.

Aum and its leader, Shōkō Asahara, were possessed by visions of the end of the world that are probably as old as death itself. Like many present-day Christian prophets of biblical world-ending events, Asahara held a belief that Armageddon would be connected to those most secular of "end time" agents—nuclear warheads or chemical and biological weapons of mass destruction.

But his cult went a step further. It undertook serious efforts to acquire and produce these weapons as part of a self-assigned project of making Armageddon happen. For the first time in history, end-time religious fanaticism allied itself with weapons capable of destroying the world, and a group embarked on the mad project of doing just that. Fortunately, much went wrong. After all, it is not so easy to destroy the world. But we have a lot to learn from the attempt.

As Asahara saw it, Armageddon, the final global conflagration, would be survived only by himself and a small band of followers, who would then create the world's "religious future." His religious standing—his status as a guru—was absolutely inseparable from this vision. Since everything was staked on it, the inference was that anything—including violence—might be called upon to ensure its arrival. Imagining a world cleansing and a new beginning has the appeal of making death both less fearful and more significant. For Aum, it meant that the world could be seen as so hopelessly polluted, so suffused with evil, as to preclude half measures.

No truth was more central to Aum than the principle that world salvation could be achieved only by bringing about the deaths of just about everyone on this earth. Disciples described their embrace of the vision and their understanding of its evolution from Hindu, Buddhist, and Christian doctrine. Asahara's idiosyncratic version of these traditions came to focus on the Buddhist concept of *poa*, which, in his distorted use, meant killing for the sake of your victims. In esoteric Buddhism, *poa* is a spiritual exercise performed when one is dying, sometimes with the aid of a guru, a "transference of consciousness" from the bodily "earth plane" to the "after-death plane" that enables one to achieve a higher realm in the next rebirth or even passage to the "Pure Land," the step prior to nirvana. Asahara came to equate murders committed by Aum members with his unusual interpretation of *poa*, in which the killer offers a benefit to the victim in a form of an improved rebirth. *Poa* became for him a core ideological principle, a theological lever for the dispensing of all existence. One can speak, then, of a weapons-hungry cult with a doctrine of altruistic murder—murder ostensibly intended to enhance the victim's immortality. The doctrine sanctified not only violence against the world at large but the killing of numerous individuals who ran afoul of the guru's aspirations.

Aum's attempts at world destruction were not, however, simply an effort to confirm the guru's own prophecy of Armageddon (though that was indeed a factor). Rather, Asahara's shifting predictions and lurid descriptions of the sequence of events by which the world would end became Aum's controlling narrative, the story that subsumed all else and into which every struggle had to fit. The narrative provided a fierce dynamic that fed hope, fear, and paranoia while never allowing either guru or disciples to rest.

Asahara was so compelling a narrator of end-of-the-world scenarios that, as one former disciple put it, listening to those stories was "like standing on top of a hill and looking down in the valley far below—and having somebody push you off." But many disciples, it could be said, had already made their own way to that cliff. Immersed as they were in the apocalyptic imagery so prominent in postwar Japanese popular culture, some of them were more or less waiting for an Asahara to give them that shove. In a society that only decades earlier had undergone an equivalent of world destruction in its abject defeat in war and its experience of having two of its cities atomically annihilated, there was a vast flow of apocalyptic narratives. Most Aum disciples, for instance, had grown up viewing a variety of futuristic daily animated television shows and reading manga (Japanese graphic novels) dramatically focused on world destruction and daring rescue missions undertaken by heroic Japanese characters. Such highly popular stories contributed to a psychological climate in which Asahara could claim absolute virtue in his war against absolute evil.

In the world of Aum, Asahara's "endism" became all-pervasive. His many-sided Armageddon constellation was the only prism through which to view the world and give it meaning, and it was increasingly bound up with Aum's immediate and growing problems. Beleaguered by mounting opposition and multiplying legal battles (mostly brought about by its own coercive and fraudulent activities), Aum struggled to hold on to its membership, and Asahara's world-ending prophecies grew ever more urgent. Armageddon became the

Losing Reality

center of a vicious circle: a sense of the end of the world impelled Aum toward, and in its eyes justified, extreme behavior
of many kinds; this extreme behavior led to inner conflict and
sometimes resistance among members that threatened the life
of the cult; that in turn brought on Aum's persecutory version
of Armageddon prophecy.

Aum is now viewed throughout the world as the primary example of the extraordinary dangers posed by private terrorist
groups arming themselves with versions of "the poor man's
atomic bomb." For Aum was a small antigovernment group
claiming ten thousand followers in Japan, about fourteen
hundred of whom were renunciants, or monks, at thirty facilities across the country; thirty thousand followers in Russia
(a figure that has been disputed); and a handful in West Germany, Sri Lanka, and the United States. Yet this relatively tiny
organization managed to manufacture, stockpile, and release
deadly sarin gas first in the city of Matsumoto, northwest
of Tokyo, and then in Tokyo itself. It also prepared equally
deadly anthrax bacillus and botulinum toxin, releasing them
several times in Tokyo and nearby areas (including in the
vicinity of two American military bases), largely unsuccessfully but with effects not yet fully known. Between 1990 and
1995 the cult staged at least fourteen chemical and biological attacks of varying dimensions. Aum also made inquiries,
particularly in Russia, into acquiring or producing nuclear
weapons. This was all part of the grandiose plan of Shōkō
Asahara to employ this weaponry to initiate World War III,
which he envisioned as a global holocaust of unprecedented

proportions that would in turn trigger a hoped-for Armageddon. In his fantasies he also saw the United States as a major military participant in this apocalyptic project.

But plans and fantasies, however earnest and elaborate, are not the same as action. A simple but terrible question therefore haunted my study of this cult: How did Aum Shinrikyō come to cross the crucial threshold from merely anticipating Armageddon to taking active steps to bring it about?

During five trips to Japan between 1995 and 1997, I was able to conduct intensive interviews with ten former members of Aum, eight men and two women, averaging more than five hours with each person. Since the guru himself and most of his leading disciples were in prison and inaccessible, the people I interviewed tended to be at either the lower- or mid-echelons of a very hierarchical organization. Only a privileged inner circle of Asahara's highest-ranking followers were told of the more violent aspects of the guru's visionary plans, and even then often incompletely. Most of those I interviewed had little or no knowledge of the various facets of Aum violence. But during their time in Aum, they had to do considerable psychological work to fend off that knowledge in the face of the evidence around them.

I focused on the inner life of Aum members, and above all on the extraordinary ramifications of the guru-disciple relationship. Most of Aum's wildly destructive visions came from its guru, but he in turn was completely dependent upon his disciples to sustain those visions and act upon them—indeed, for his own psychological functioning. One can understand little about Aum without probing the extremity of what can be called its guruism, and that guruism helps us to grasp certain essential aspects of the leader-follower interaction in much of the extreme behavior taking place elsewhere. Included in Aum's guruism was a bizarre embrace of science to "prove" Aum's religious truths and to provide Asahara with the kinds of ultimate weapons that might bring such "truths" to fruition.

One can look at the guru of a fanatical new religion or cult as either everything or nothing. The "everything" would acknowledge the guru's creation of his group and its belief system, as well as his sustained control over it—in which case the bizarre behavior of Aum Shinrikyō could be understood as little more than a reflection of Shōkō Asahara's own bizarre ideas and emotions. The "nothing" would suggest that the guru is simply a creation of the hungers of his disciples, that he has no existence apart from his disciples, that any culture can produce psychological types like him, that without disciples, there is no guru. Both views have elements of truth, but the deeper truth lies in combining them, in seizing upon the paradox.

Gurus and disciples are inevitably products of a particular historical moment. They represent a specific time and place, even as they draw upon ancient psychological and theological themes. As our contemporaries, this group was like the rest of us psychologically unmoored, adrift from and often confused about older value systems and traditions. That unmoored state has great importance. Here I would stress only that a guru's complete structural and psychological separateness from a traditional cultural institution—in Asahara's case an established religion—permits him to improvise wildly in both his theology and his personal behavior, to become a "floating guru." Disciples in turn are open to any strange direction he may lead them and contribute their own unmoored fantasies without the restraining force that a religious or institutional hierarchy might provide.

The British psychoanalyst Anthony Storr offers a useful description of a guru type: a spiritual teacher whose insight is based on personal revelation, often taking the form of a vision understood to come directly from a deity. The revelation, which has transformed his life, generally follows upon a period of distress or illness in his thirties or forties. There is suddenly a sense of certainty, of having found "the truth," creating a general aura around him that "he knows." The emerging guru can then promise, as Asahara did, "new ways of self-development, new paths to salvation, always generalizing from [his] own experience."

As such, the narrative of the guru—of the religious founder in general—can be seen as a version of the myth of the hero. That myth involves a mysterious birth and early childhood, a call to greatness, and a series of ordeals and trials culminating in heroic achievement. I believe that this culmination lies in the hero's achievement of special knowledge of, or mastery over, death, which can in turn enhance the life of his people. In the case of the religious hero—the guru—the ordeals faced must be moral and spiritual; the crux of the guru biography, therefore, is the overcoming of moral failure by means of spiritual rebirth.

Asahara entered readily into that myth by means of conscious manipulation as well as unconscious inclination. He claimed that he had reached enlightenment and seems to have been convinced, in at least a part of his mind, that he had indeed become enlightened and that his spiritual achievement entitled—even required—him to be a great guru or perhaps a deity. Over time he became the charismatic guru with long, flowing hair and beard, and as time went on, he also began to dress in the flowing purple robes that suggested a Hindu holy man.

"Guru" is not a title that is used in much Japanese religious practice. It is a Sanskrit word meaning "heavy," suggesting a person of special weight. The guru's authority is such that he is sometimes described as "Father-Mother." In the original Hindu tradition he is more important to the Brahman (a member of the Hindu priestly caste) than the Brahman's actual parents because the latter merely "bring him into existence" while "the birth of a Brahman to a Veda (sacred knowledge) lasts forever." The *Tibetan Book of the Dead* describes three kinds of gurus: ordinary religious teachers who are part of the "human line"; more-extraordinary human beings possessed of special spiritual powers; and "superhuman" beings of the "heavenly (or 'divine') line." Asahara was to claim to be all three.

Even in its early years, Aum Shinrikyō showed signs of extreme guruism, intense apocalypticism, and the violent potential in both. Asahara was spoken of and addressed as *Sonshi*, meaning "revered master" or "exalted one," a highly worshipful term not ordinarily used in Japanese Buddhism.

A disciple came to understand that without the guru nothing was possible, but with him there opened up a path to perfection and to reincarnations in higher realms. It was expected that the disciple would not only surrender himself to the guru but "merge" or "fuse" with him. He was to become what Asahara in one of his sermons spoke of as a "clone" of the guru.

Asahara recruited scientists more actively than he did any other group. His enthusiasm about science undoubtedly was connected with his lust for murderous weapons. But the guru also wished to consider himself a scientist and once declared, "A religion which cannot be scientifically proven is fake." He was especially interested in brainwaves and claimed that by studying them Aum could establish a scientific basis for the stages of spiritual attainment described by past Buddhist saints. With the help of Hideo Murai, Asahara's chief scientist, Aum introduced the use of a headset that purportedly contained the guru's brain waves, which it transmitted to the disciple in a procedure known as the "perfect salvation initiation." The PSI, much revered in Aum, was meant to bring about the desired "cloning" of the guru by means of technology and science. In this way science readily became pseudoscience, or simply fantasy. There was also a strong element of science fiction in the PSI and other Aum projects, much of it actively fed by television programs. What took shape in Aum was a blending of science occultism and science fiction, with little distinction between the fictional and the actual.

Among Asahara's most crucial early decisions was the creation of *shukke*, or renunciants. *Shukke* means "leaving home" and is a traditional term for monks or nuns who give up the world. Aum's message was that if one really wished to follow the guru and join in his full spiritual project, one had to become a *shukke*, removing oneself completely from one's family and one's prior work or study and turning all one's resources— money, property, and self—over to Aum and its guru. Even one's name was to be abandoned, replaced by a Sanskrit one. Such a renunciation of the world in favor of life in a small, closed society is the antithesis of the this-worldly emphasis of most Japanese religious practice and a repudiation of the still-powerful hold the Japanese family has over its members. As a family-like alternative to an actual family's conflicts and confusions, however, it proved a definite attraction to many young people.

Living together in Aum facilities, *shukke* underwent severe forms of ascetic practice, including celibacy and a prohibition against ejaculation, fasting, long hours of meditation, intense breathing exercises, and vigorous sequences of prostration combined with demanding work assignments and irregular sleep (often only a few hours a night). Their existence was a Spartan one—two meals a day of extremely simple "Aum food" (rice and vegetables), tiny sleeping spaces, and no personal possessions. The fervent atmosphere was further heightened by Aum's gradual adoption of a series of initiations. In addition to PSI, there was *shaktipat*, in which the guru mobilized a disciple's energy by touching his chakra points, or energy centers, on the forehead or top of the head; there was a "*bardo* initiation" (named for the "in-between state" connecting death and rebirth), in which the initiate was brought before the "Lord of Hell" to hear accusations about his lifelong misbehaviors (the accusations sometimes rendered more specific by information previously obtained with the help of narcotic drugs administered to the initiate); a "Christ initiation," in which the guru or a high disciple would personally offer the initiate a liquid containing LSD to help evoke visions; a "narco initiation," in which a narcotic drug was used to extract a confession; and a "resolve initiation," in which, again with the use of a narcotic drug, the initiate was required to chant repeatedly his failure to absorb Aum's full message and his determination to make greater efforts to do so in the future. As guru, Asahara retained his own sexual privileges in what was in principle an otherwise celibate community, continuing to live with his wife and family, taking on long-term mistresses from among Aum disciples, and offering tantric sexual initiations, or "transfers of energy," to various female followers.

Aum's environment was one of intense ideological totalism, in which everything had to be experienced on an all-or-nothing basis. Within that totalism Aum disciples could thrive. They could embrace the extremity of the cult's ascetism as a proud discipline that gave new meaning to their lives. Above all, they could repeatedly experience altered states of consciousness, what in Aum were known as "mystical experiences." These too had a characteristic pattern: light-headedness followed by a sense of the mind leaving the body, the appearance of white or colored lights, and sometimes images either of the Buddha or of the guru. Such altered states resulted from intense forms of religious practice—especially from the oxygen deprivation brought about by yogic rapid-breathing exercises—and, later on, from the use of drugs like LSD. But they were all attributed to the guru's unique spiritual power and so were considered indicators of one's own spiritual progress. There was nothing more important to disciples than to hold on to these mystical experiences, for which purpose they could numb themselves to immediate evidence of violence around them—or join in that violence.

There was considerable violence even in the training procedures to which disciples could be subjected: protracted immersion in extremely hot or cold water, hanging by one's feet for hours at a time, or solitary confinement for days in a tiny cell-like room that had no facilities and could become unbearably hot. Though the distinction between training and punishment often blurred, these procedures were justified by the need of the disciple to overcome the bad karma he or she brought to Aum or, in the phrase commonly used in the cult, to "drop karma."

Asahara's tendencies toward megalomania required, and were fed by, his disciples' infinite adulation. Over the years that the interaction was sustained, one can speak of the guru's functional megalomania. He presented himself to the world as civilization's greatest spiritual figure—an embodiment of Shiva, the Buddha, and Christ—and as a genius in virtually every field of human endeavor. In addition, there were claims that he possessed nirvana-like brain waves, blood with special properties that could be transmitted to disciples who drank it, and a unique and distinctive form of DNA. Within the cult his megalomania was made manifest through his claim to spiritual omniscience and to having control over everyone's bad karma. The megalomania also drew Asahara to weapons of ultimate destruction, the possession of which in turn fed and enhanced that mental state.

But as we have mentioned earlier, the guru needs disciples not only to become and remain a guru but to hold himself together psychologically. For the guru self often teeters on the edge of fragmentation, paranoia, and overall psychological breakdown. We can observe a particularly bizarre and violent version of this in Asahara, and in the manner in which he disintegrated when his closest disciples turned against him.

Toward the demise of the group, as Asahara's control over his environment faltered, his megalomania ceased to be functional. Threats from the outside (groups contesting Aum's activities and the developing police investigation of its murders) and from the inside (insufficient numbers of renunciants and strains in guru-disciple relationships) undermined the shared fantasy so necessary to the workings of such megalomania. The guru's intensified paranoia drove him toward external violence as well as toward various forms of self-destruction, and he became more extreme and fragmented.

Two months after the sarin attack, the police found Shōkō Asahara in a small hidden cubicle in Aum headquarters dressed in his purple priestly robes, lying in his urine, and surrounded by piles of Japanese currency totaling about ten million yen. A kind of de-guruizing process—and the subversion of whatever functional megalomania remained—began when the police gave him orders that he had to obey, and ignored his insistence that "no one is allowed to touch the guru's body." Legal authorities further negated Asahara's guruhood by denying him the right to appear in court in his priestly robes, stating that these had "religious meaning" and could influence witnesses who had been or were still cult members.

Little of his functional megalomania survived his relegation to the status of prisoner subject to the will and demands of others. Perhaps the final assault on his megalomanic guru identity, however, was the humiliating defection of former high disciples who not only implicated him in the sarin attacks and various individual murders but, much worse for him psychologically, mocked his spiritual claims. In open court, for instance, Shigeo Sugimoto, a leading member of Aum's inner circle, declared, "I was deceived by the claim that the guru was a person who had achieved final liberation." The idea of Asahara's taking on other people's karma was "complete nonsense"; instead, "he sought to satisfy his own desires." Sugimoto now saw the guru as a "foolish human being" who had nevertheless managed to use him.

In the fall of 1996, after a series of confrontations in court with angry and accusatory former disciples, Asahara's megalomanic, totalized self appeared to break down altogether. The moment of dramatic shift seemed to occur when Yoshihiro Inoue, perhaps his closest disciple, began detailing in court Asahara's full role in directing the sarin attack. As he testified, making clear his complete rejection of Aum's founder by calling him a "false guru," Asahara showed signs of what was described in newspaper reports as "mental instability" and on several occasions had to be removed from the courtroom. In short, his megalomanic immortality system was shattered.

Crossing the Threshold

Thus far, I have been trying to describe the behavior and motivations of Aum Shinrikyō's members in their bizarre foray into world-ending violence. Now I want to identify the central characteristics that contributed to its collective dynamic as lived out by the guru and his disciples. Exploring them may put us in a better position to answer the question posed at the beginning of this study: How did Aum cross the threshold from anticipating to forcing Armageddon?

None of the seven characteristics I will cite is unique to Aum, but Aum distinguished itself from similar groups in the way it combined them and in the degree of totalism it brought to this extremely dangerous mix. Other groups elsewhere may in the future be all too capable of doing what Aum did, and more. Whatever group might next embark on world destruction is likely to possess versions of most or all of these characteristics.

The first characteristic of Aum was *totalized guruism*, which became *paranoid guruism* and *megalomanic guruism*. Instead of awakening the potential of his disciples, Shōkō Asahara himself became his cult's only source of "energy" or infinite life-power and its only source of the new self that each Aum disciple was expected to acquire (as epitomized by the religious name every disciple took as a renunciant). For the disciples there was no deity beyond the guru, no ethical code beyond his demands and imposed ordeals. When the guru invoked a higher deity it was only in order to incorporate the god's omnipotence into his own. Guru and disciples were both energized and entrapped by their claim to ultimate existential truth and virtue.

This megalomanic guruism, the claim to possess and control immediate and distant reality, was not only wild fantasy but a form of de-symbolization—a loss, that is, of the symbolizing function that characterizes the healthy human mind. The guru took on a stance beyond metaphor. He could no longer, in the words of Martin Buber, "imagine the real." Wendy Doniger, a scholar of Hinduism, points out that most mythology consists of concrete narration in the service of metaphor, of descriptions of behavior meant to suggest, rather than express, primal human emotions and dilemmas. In reading mythological stories, we seek to reconnect their concrete details to the symbolized, metaphorical world in which we exist psychologically. A megalomanic guru like Asahara does the reverse: he embraces the very concreteness of mythic narratives so as to circumvent the metaphor and symbolization so crucial to the functioning human imagination.

This de-symbolization became bound up with a second Aum characteristic: *a vision of an apocalyptic event or series of events that would destroy the world in the service of renewal.* All great religions contain variations of that vision, ordinarily causing followers to struggle with its symbolic meanings. Asahara, who frequently cited the god Shiva as a source of inspiration and personal connection to the divine, did not engage in this struggle such matters as Shiva's dancing the world out of existence so that it might be renewed. That "dance," as one commentator puts it, "is only an allusion," a way to represent powerful human forces, in this case a grandiose version of the great universal myth of death and rebirth, of world destruction and re-creation. Even the early Hindu storytellers, in shaping the myth, warned that much of the detail was meant to be suggestive and timeless rather than literal and prescriptive. But the megalomanic guru absorbed the myth totally into his world-encompassing self so that he could claim to act for and *as* Shiva in embarking on a concrete contemporary project of world destruction and renewal.

A third Aum characteristic was its *ideology of killing to heal, of altruistic murder and altruistic world destruction*. Such a stance readily evoked an "attack guruism" and an "action prophecy" directed toward forcing the end. The concept of *poa*, as manipulated by Asahara, epitomized this stance, encouraging as it did the killing of a spiritually inferior person by a spiritually superior one for the sake of improving the prospects of immortality for both. In Aum, the principle of killing to heal extended into a vision of altruistic omnicide. The more I studied Aum's medical behavior, the more I was reminded of the experience of Nazi doctors and of the more general potential of doctors to replace healing with killing in the service of a movement or cause. Like the Nazis, Aum put forth a medical ideology that claimed radical ethical advances. With Aum, the ethical claim was highly spiritualized, and could be understood as a medicalized projection of ultimate guruism, a spiritually sanitized version of what was to become medicalized killing.

This altruistic mass murder depended, in turn, on a fourth characteristic: *the relentless impulse toward world-rejecting purification*. Aum drew upon its version of karma as ubiquitous defilement. Asahara was once quoted as saying that "the essence of the devil is matter," suggesting that what Aum had to "purify" was physical existence itself. Such an unrealizable purification goal kept Aum disciples on a spiritual treadmill in the service of the guru and of a process that was envisioned as transhistorical. Asahara sought, or claimed to seek, a level of eternal perfection that defied the petty external standards of any particular era; yet he didn't hesitate to apply his standards of purification to the most immediate social and political behavior. Disciples were strongly drawn to his compelling rendition of the many corruptions of contemporary society, already vivid in their experience and observations. Aum's radical rejection of the world as impure and evil spoke persuasively to powerful feelings of alienation in young potential cult members, just as the cult's radical eschatology spoke directly to the broader apocalyptic mood of a society that within living memory had received a taste of what a world-ending event might actually be like.

A fifth characteristic of Aum was the *lure of ultimate weapons*. If Asahara's consciousness of nuclear weapons was initially related to Hiroshima and Nagasaki, ultimate weapons in general became bound up with his action prophecy in pressing toward Armageddon. For Asahara it was an easy and natural path from nuclearism to dreams of mass killing via chemical and biological devices. Crucial to his pursuit of mass murder was the fact that he was a "floating guru," unencumbered by a restraining god, by a restraining code of traditional values, or even, as a state might be, by the interests of an entrenched

bureaucracy. As they did for the United States and the Soviet Union during the Cold War, weapons of mass death increasingly took their place at the center of Aum's structure
and function. Aum was the first nongovernmental religious
or political cult to achieve this kind of weapons involvement,
but it is unlikely to be the last. For such weapons have come to
affect human consciousness everywhere and are bound to remain a powerful lure to totalistically inclined, paranoid, and
megalomanic gurus.

Essential to success in Aum's killing project was a sixth
characteristic: *a shared state of aggressive numbing*. That mental state began with a disciple's merger with the guru, with
the ideal of becoming his clone and of thinking and feeling
as he did. Vajrayāna, a form of Buddhism that Asahara drew
from, which in Sanskrit means "Diamond Vehicle," was interpreted by Asahara to signify, among other things, pursuit of
a "diamond mind" that could be calm, stable, and detached
from worldly concerns. Achieving such a "diamond mind,"
or what Aum called a "sacred carefree mind," could involve
fierce dedication to forms of "spiritual practice" that included
extreme asceticism, cruelty, and murder. Such dedication was
a form of numbing, which one enhanced by an absolute focus
on the violent attack immediately at hand, on one's efficacy
in carrying it out; a focus that could sweep away past scruples
as well as any empathy for potential victims. The principle of
viewing the guru's most outrageous demands as an appropriate form of personal ordeal or "test" reinforced the numbing
process and resulted in a mental state similar to that cultivated
among Japanese soldiers during World War II. In serving the

emperor—in essence a distant but highly venerated guru—
the soldier was to steel his mind against all compunctions or
feelings of compassion, to achieve, that is, a version of the "diamond mind" that could contribute both to fanatical fighting
and to grotesque acts of atrocity.

A seventh characteristic of Aum was its *extreme techno-
cratic manipulation*, coupled with its *claim to absolute scientific truth*. Aum held to a computer theory of the mind: the
principles of replacing "bad data" from the culture with "good
data" from the guru. The cult's entire effort at spiritual self-
transformation was, in fact, reduced to systematic techniques,
whether in the form of breathing exercises, drug-centered
initiations, or endless repetitions of the guru's words or his
assigned mantras. Practitioners were given specific technical
functions to perform—running businesses, doing translations, making publishing arrangements, creating artwork,
composing or playing music, working in Aum "factories,"
preparing chemical or biological weapons, drawing up legal
contracts—always as cogs in a larger machine of "salvation."
Spiritual experiences were ultimately relegated to their com-
partmentalized function within that Aum machine. Guru and
cult constantly pressed for the technological means of achieving faster salvation, whether better drugs for disciples' visions
or more effective ultimate weapons for inducing Armageddon. In these and other ways, Aum followed the tendency of
totalistic cults to create a "sacred science" and thereby bring
two ultimate claims to truth together in a single omnipotent
package.

Aum also demonstrated the bizarre consequences of the

fanatical conversion of scientists to totalistic guruism, of what might be called megalomanic science. One cannot ignore the extent of Aum's success—despite its scientific and technological bungling—with its weaponry or the deadly consequences it wrought turning scientific energies to the service of religious fanaticism. In merging the two, Aum made a grotesque pioneering foray into the most dangerous of all contemporary imaginative combinations.

We must face Aum's significance for the human future and ponder the question of how to deal with, and what alternatives there might be to, its vision of apocalyptic violence. For Aum was about death in the nuclear age, about a distorted passion for survival, and about an ever more desperate quest for immortality. It was also about despising the world so much that one feels impelled to destroy it. In these ways, Aum encompassed the most destructive forces of the twentieth century.

Although Aum was Japanese, there was hardly a religious tradition or geographical region—from Russia to Australia, India to the United States—that Asahara did not ransack for the components of his spirituality, his weapons systems, and his rationale for mass murder. Conversely, there are impulses closely related to Asahara's found in each of these regions and their spiritual traditions. And given the expanding availability of ultimate weapons, no national boundaries can contain those who are bent on forcing the end. In fact, the capability of doing so is likely to descend to ever smaller, more driven, and more technologically sophisticated groups. Aum Shinrikyō demonstrated, in however bungling a manner, that the potential initiation of such world-threatening destruction could be mounted by a small cult combining zealotry and weaponry. Aum, in other words, may have been a kind of bellwether, an indicator of future trends.

For all these reasons Aum should be seen not as an end point but as a threatening beginning, an expression of a new dimension of global danger. There is no lack of hunger in groups throughout the world for absolute moral clarity—not just for a leader but for a guru or savior—and of a sense that only the most extreme measures can bring about a yearned-for transformation of existence. Nor does there seem to be any lack of prospective gurus or saviors ready to emerge from such social climates. They, in turn, require disciples in order to cope with their own profound vulnerabilities. Everywhere there are potential gurus and potential disciples longing to be, in William James's phrase, "melted into unity." Their hungers are sustained by the imagery of annihilation, whether involving weaponry or the destruction of the human habitat, what we misleadingly call "our environment."

It is highly unlikely that the Aum Shinrikyō experience will simply repeat itself, in Japan or elsewhere, but quite likely that Aum-like traits will coalesce in groups as yet unknown to us. We do well to reconsider, with Asahara and Aum in mind, the American cultic landscape and its global interactions. To be sure, there is no certainty at all that the next urge to force the end will take threatening form in the United States as opposed to, say, post-Communist Russia, the Middle East, or the Indian subcontinent. But the United States has been a particularly fertile environment for cults. Examining a few American cults of recent times through the prism of Shōkō Asahara can deepen our understanding of cultic phenomena and our thinking about possible futures as well. Certainly, several of our most sensational cults—the Charles Manson Family, Jim Jones's Peoples Temple, and Marshall Herff Applewhite's Heaven's Gate—take on a different aspect in the wake of Aum. The same is true of the cultic milieu of the present-day extreme right, where fantasies of using weapons of mass destruction to transform and purify the world are powerfully present.

6

Nazi Doctors

For the Nazis, biological purification became sacralized. The whole Nazi project was apocalyptic and cultist, with Hitler the murderous guru. Nazi cultism in turn suggested the cultism of genocide.

Nazi millennialism, as expressed in the vision of the "thousand-year Reich," has parallels with the Chinese Communist slogan "May the revolutionary regime stay red for ten thousand generations." We see here a secular manifestation of the Christian vision of Christ returning for a thousand-year reign on earth, a secular manifestation of an apocalyptic vision of "end times." There is much evidence to suggest that this biological purification was the ultimate motivation of Nazi behavior, the major source of invasion and occupation of other countries and of mass murder. Biology became mystified as a path to curing the ills of the Nordic race and ultimately purifying the world. This mystical dimension was expressed to me by the doctor who was so moved by a high Nazi official's declaration that "National Socialism is nothing but applied biology," that he joined the Party the next day. All this was part of what I came to call the Nazi "biomedical vision," which found its culminating expression in Auschwitz.

Most German doctors at Auschwitz were not extreme ideologues but were socialized to killing, meaning that they sufficiently internalized the morals and behavior of the group to which they were assigned. This was a medical version of what Raul Hilberg, the great Holocaust scholar, called the bureaucratization of killing and what Hannah Arendt was later to call the "banality of evil." Concerning the latter, I tried to make it clear that, while the men were banal, the evil they perpetrated was not, and also that over time they became less banal in their sustained participation in killing. Nevertheless, they were professionals who participated all too actively in the malignant normality of Auschwitz; they did what was expected of them in selecting Jews for the gas chambers and supervising the killing process.

That malignant normality was established, disseminated, and institutionalized by Hitler and his early followers. There was the ideological claim that the Nordic race alone was a culture-creating race; other races could sustain but not create culture; and the Jewish "race" was a destroyer of culture. The power of the Nordic race had been undermined by Jewish influence, and that influence had to be removed for the Nordic race to regain its health and greatness. In that sense, the destruction of Jews was a therapeutic necessity.

A minority of doctors could express their own fanaticism, as in the case of one who, when asked how he could reconcile the gas chambers with his Hippocratic oath, replied: "Of course I am a doctor and I want to preserve life. And out of respect for human life, I would remove a gangrenous appendix from a diseased body. The Jew is the gangrenous appendix in the body of mankind." These views and policies were buttressed by an all-pervasive concept of "life unworthy of life," a concept that didn't originate with the Nazis but was one they embraced to justify their sequence of actions starting from coercive sterilization to the direct medical killing of the "euthanasia" project to the mass killing of the death camps.

This biomedical vision was part of a more general mysticism that was as described to me and observed firsthand by an American psychiatric colleague, Albert Stunkard, who, as a schoolboy, lived in Germany during the 1930s because his father's scientific fellowship had brought the family there. Stunkard was astounded by the behavior of many of his student friends; formerly serious and rational adolescents, they became ecstatic Nazi supporters at rallies and in their everyday demeanor. Their intense idealism seemed to him to be transformed into a mystical sense of being part of a new movement that gave meaning to their lives and promise to the human future. (Stunkard was to learn, with some sadness, that most of his friends were eventually killed in military combat.) The larger truth here is that movements that kill great numbers of people are likely to do so with the claim to virtue—and that virtue tends to be, as it was here, one of purification and healing.

Of course, the Nazi movement was unique in terms of its killing machines and its policy of rounding up millions of people in order to systematically murder them. Nonetheless, the Nazi form of cultism has close resemblances to that of other political and religious groups, and leaves no doubt about cultist capacities for infinite murderousness.

The Nazi Doctors
First published in 1986

When we think of the crimes of Nazi doctors, what come to mind are their cruel and sometimes fatal human experiments. Those experiments, in their precise and absolute violation of the Hippocratic oath, mock and subvert the very idea of the ethical physician, of the physician dedicated to the well-being of patients. Yet when we turn to the Nazi doctor's role in Auschwitz, it was not the experiments that were most significant. Rather, it was his participation in the killing process—indeed his supervision of Auschwitz mass murder from beginning to end. This medicalized killing had a logic that was not only deeply significant for Nazi theory and behavior but holds for other expressions of genocide as well.

At the heart of this process was the transformation of the physician—of the medical enterprise itself—from healer to killer. That transformation requires us to examine the interaction of Nazi political ideology and biomedical ideology in their effects on individual and collective behavior. Throughout this study I struggled with the disturbing psychological truth that participation in mass murder need not require emotions as extreme or demonic as would seem appropriate for such a malignant project. I was struck by the ordinariness of most Nazi doctors I interviewed. Neither brilliant nor stupid, neither inherently evil nor particularly ethically sensitive, they were by no means the demonic figures—sadistic, fanatic, lusting to kill—people have often thought them to be. But that did not mean that Nazi doctors were faceless bureaucratic cogs or automatons. As human beings, they were actors and participants who manifested certain kinds of behavior for which they were responsible, and which we can begin to identify. While a few doctors resisted the nazification of the medical profession, and some had little sympathy for the Nazis, as a profession German physicians offered themselves to the regime.

The medicalized killing during the Nazi regime can be understood in two broad perspectives. The first is the "surgical" method of killing large numbers of people by means of a controlled technology making use of highly poisonous gas; the method employed became a means of maintaining distance between killers and victims. This distancing had considerable importance for the Nazis in alleviating the psychological problems experienced (as attested over and over by Nazi documents) by the *Einsatzgruppen* troops who carried out face-to-face shooting of Jews in Eastern Europe (though these problems did not prevent them from murdering 1.4 million Jews).

But there is another perspective on medicalized killing that I believe to be insufficiently recognized: *killing as a therapeutic imperative*. Pre-Hitler ideologues as well as Hitler himself interpreted Germany's post–First World War chaos and demoralization as an "illness," especially of the Aryan race. Hitler wrote in *Mein Kampf*, in the mid-1920s, that "anyone who wants to cure this era, which is inwardly sick and rotten, must first of all summon up the courage to make clear the causes of this disease." The diagnosis was racial. The only genuine "culture-creating" race, the Aryans, had permitted themselves to be weakened to the point of endangered survival by the "destroyers of culture," characterized as "the Jew." The Jews were agents of "racial pollution" and "racial tuberculosis," as well as parasites and bacteria causing sickness, deterioration, and death in the host peoples they infested. According to Hitler, "If . . . the Jew conquers the nations of this world, his crown will become the funeral wreath of humanity, and once again this planet, empty of mankind, will move through the ether as it did thousands of years ago." That is, the Jews would destroy not only the Aryan race, but everyone and everything else. With so absolute and so ultimate a threat, genocide became not only appropriate but an urgent necessity. The cure had to be radical and biological: that is (as one scholar put it), by "cutting out the 'canker of decay,' propagating the worthwhile elements and letting the less valuable wither away, . . . [and] 'the extirpation of all those categories of people considered to be worthless or dangerous.'"

In *Mein Kampf*, Hitler declared the sacred racial mission of the German people to be "assembling and preserving the most valuable stocks of basic racial elements [and] . . . slowly and surely raising them to a dominant position." He was specific about the necessity for sterilization ("the most modern medical means") on behalf of an immortalizing vision of the state-mediated race ("a millennial future"). And for him the stakes were absolute: "If the power to fight for one's own health is no longer present, the right to live in this world of struggle ends." Thus, the unifying principle of the Nazi biomedical ideology was that of a deadly racial disease, the sickness of the Aryan race; the cure, the killing of all Jews.

Hitler's immortalizing racial vision was connected to the Nazi concept of the *Volk*—a term not only denoting "people" but conveying for many German thinkers "the union of a group of people with a transcendental 'essence' . . . [which] might be called 'nature' or 'cosmos' or 'mythos,' but in each instance . . . was fused to man's innermost nature, and represented the source of his creativity, his depth of feeling, his individuality, and his unity with other members of the *Volk*." We may say that *Volk* came to embody an immortalizing connection with eternal racial and cultural substance. And that connection begins to put us in touch with the Nazi version of "revolutionary immortality."

The Nazis themselves can be understood as a vast millennial cult, projecting what they called "the thousand-year Reich" while engaging regularly in pagan religious rituals, especially at large party rallies (depicted in the powerfully disturbing film *Triumph of the Will*). Within Nazi ideology, Nazi doctors were cast as shamanistic figures in a vastly murderous cultic process. We may say that the doctor standing at the ramp in Auschwitz represented a kind of omega point, a mythical gatekeeper between the worlds of the dead and the living, a final common pathway of the Nazi vision of therapy via mass murder. Always at issue for the medical profession was its role in protecting and revitalizing the genetic health of the *Volk*.

The Nazi project had a vision of absolute control over the evolutionary process, over the biological human future. Making widespread use of the Darwinian term "selection," the Nazis sought to take over the functions of nature (natural selection) and God ("the Lord giveth and the Lord taketh away") in orchestrating their own "selections," their own version of human evolution. In their principle of taking over evolution from nature in order to prevent humanity from being "annihilated by degeneration," the Nazis were putting forward their sweeping version of biological—one might say evolutionary—purification. Once doctors themselves had undergone purification (Hitler stressed the "cleansing" of the medical profession—which meant getting rid of Jews and political opponents—so that it could assume "racial leadership"), they became the professional purifiers. They now were the "alert biological soldiers" on guard against anything strange or deficient and therefore defiling with its contagion. Scientific racism and mental hygiene were the medical-materialistic principles by which the Nazis murdered in the name of purification. Above all, one had to "purify the blood," which became a means of rendering sacred the mystical-immortal Aryan race and community.

Physician-biologists saw themselves as the core of the mystical body of the *Volk*. One doctor's term for his biological mysticism was "biological socialism." The Nazis, he insisted, had been able to bring together nationalism and socialism because of their "recognition of the natural phenomena of life." Here we may say that mysticism, especially communal mysticism, was given a biological and medical face. Each Nazi doctor was to be a biological militant living under "the great idea of the National Socialist biological state structure."

Hitler understood himself to be a prophet whose racial vision outdistanced the state's structure, making it necessary for him to avoid the bureaucratic apparatus and proceed directly to the matter at hand. One way of doing that was to go straight to the doctors. Inevitably, he ended up creating an elaborate new bureaucracy, one that was both medical and murderous. One can speak of the Nazi state as a "biocracy." The model here is a theocracy, a system of rule by priests of a sacred order under the claim of divine prerogative. In the case of the Nazi biocracy, the divine prerogative was that of cure through purification and revitalization of the Aryan race. And just as in a theocracy, the state itself was no more than a vehicle for the divine purpose.

Medical metaphor blended with concrete biomedical ideology in the Nazi sequence from coercive sterilization to direct medical killing to the death camps. The Nazis based their justification for direct medical killing on the simple concept of "life unworthy of life" (*lebensunwertes Leben*). While the Nazis did not originate this concept, they carried it to its ultimate biological, racial, and "therapeutic" extreme. Of the five identifiable steps by which the Nazis carried out the principle of "life unworthy of life," coercive sterilization was the first. Establishing widespread compulsory sterilization became a sacred mission. The genetic romanticism of an extreme biomedical vision was combined with a totalistic political structure to enable the nation to carry out relentlessly, and without legal interference, a more extensive program of compulsory sterilization than had ever previously been attempted. These sterilization policies were always associated with the therapeutic and regenerative principles of the biomedical vision: the "purification of the national body" and the "eradication of morbid hereditary dispositions." Indeed, the entire Nazi regime was built on a biomedical vision that *required* the kind of racial purification that would progress from sterilization to extensive killing. No one really knows how many people were actually sterilized; reliable estimates are generally between 200,000 and 350,000.

After the program of coercive sterilization, the Nazis established a policy of direct medical killing—that is, killing arranged within medical channels, by means of medical decisions, and carried out by doctors and their assistants. The Nazis called this program "euthanasia." Since, for them, this term camouflaged mass murder, I have chosen to enclose it within quotation marks when referring to that program. "Euthanasia" began with the killing of "impaired" children in hospitals, and moved on to the killing of "impaired" adults, mostly collected from mental hospitals, in centers especially equipped with carbon monoxide gas. This project was extended (in the same killing centers) to "impaired" inmates of concentration and extermination camps and, finally, to mass killings, mostly of Jews, in the extermination camps themselves. In the concentration camps, the "life unworthy of life" designation eventually included all groups considered by the regime to be undesirable (Jews, homosexuals, political opponents, ordinary criminals, "shiftless elements," Catholic critics, and so on.)

Had the Nazis named their "euthanasia" institutions according to their concepts, they might well have referred to the "Hartheim [or Grafeneck] Center for Therapeutic Genetic Killing" and, correspondingly, to the "Auschwitz Center for Therapeutic Racial Killing." In Auschwitz, Nazi doctors presided over the murder of most of the one million victims of that camp. Doctors performed selections—both on the ramp among arriving transports of prisoners and later in the camps and on the medical blocks. Doctors supervised the killing in the gas chambers and decided when the victims were dead. Doctors conducted a murderous epidemiology, sending to the gas chamber groups of people with contagious diseases and sometimes including everyone else who might be on the medical block. Doctors ordered and supervised, and at times carried out, direct killing of debilitated patients on the medical blocks by means of phenol injections into the bloodstream or the heart. In connection with all of these killings, doctors kept up a pretense of medical legitimacy: for deaths of Auschwitz prisoners and of outsiders brought there to be killed, they signed false death certificates listing spurious illnesses (as they had also done in connection with "euthanasia" killings). Doctors consulted actively on how best to keep selections running smoothly; on how many people to permit to remain alive to fill the slave labor requirements of the I. G. Farben enterprise at Auschwitz; and on how to burn the enormous numbers of bodies that strained the facilities of the crematoria.

To perform selections, the Nazi doctor had to make the psychic shift from ideology to actual mass murder. Doctors could call forth an absolutized Nazi version of good and evil as both justification for what they were seeing and doing and for further avoidance of its psychological actuality. And by viewing the whole matter as a problem that needed to be "solved," by whatever means, that pragmatic goal could become the only focus.

But the key to understanding how Nazi doctors came to do the work of Auschwitz is the psychological principle I call "doubling": the division of the self into two functioning wholes, so that a part-self acts as an entire self. An Auschwitz doctor could through doubling not only kill and contribute to killing but also organize silently, on behalf of that evil project, an entire self-structure (or self-process) encompassing virtually all aspects of his behavior.

Doubling is an active psychological process, a means of adaptation to extremity. Auschwitz as an institution—as an atrocity-producing situation—ran on doubling. An atrocity-producing situation is one so structured externally (in this case, institutionally) that the average person entering it (in this case, as part of the German authority) will commit or become associated with atrocities. Always important to an atrocity-producing situation is its capacity to motivate individuals psychologically toward engaging in atrocity. Beyond

Auschwitz, there was much in the Nazi movement that promoted doubling. The overall Nazi project, replete with cruelty, required constant doubling in the service of carrying out that cruelty. Doubling could also be more dramatic, infused with transcendence, the sense of being someone entering a religious order "who must now divest himself of his past," and of being "reborn into a new European race." That new Nazi self could take on a sense of mystical fusion with the German *Volk*, with "destiny," and with immortalizing powers. One was asked to double in Auschwitz on behalf of revitalization that was communal (with doctors the racial mediators between the hero leader and the larger Aryan community) and sacred (claiming its ultimate sanction from the dead of the First World War).

Selections, the quintessential Auschwitz ritual, epitomized and maintained the healing-killing paradox. The first selections performed by the arriving SS doctor were his ritual of initiation, his transition from ordinary life to the Auschwitz universe, and the early calling forth of his Auschwitz self. Like most functioning rituals, selections became regularized over time, as the Auschwitz self became established and more experienced. The regime drew much of its power from its ritualization of existence, so that every act it called forth could be seen as having profound mythic significance for the "Third Reich" and the "Aryan race."

The Nazi ethos thus came to contain a sacred biology, whose logic was taken on and actively promulgated by the Auschwitz self. For the claim of logic and rationality was part of the larger Nazi claim of direct outgrowth from the principles of biology. To be sure, other movements—Marxism and Soviet Communism, for instance—have also claimed scientific validity. But only the Nazis have seen themselves as products and practitioners of the science of life and life processes—as biologically ordained guides to their own and the world's biological destiny. Whatever their hubris, and whatever the elements of pseudoscience and scientism in what they actually did, they identified themselves with the science of their time. That logic of science was always, at least in Nazi eyes, close at hand, and the Auschwitz self could feel a certain national-scientific tradition behind its harsh, apocalyptic, deadly rationality.

Genocide

The behavior of Nazi doctors suggests the beginnings of a psychology of genocide. Rather than a definitive theory of genocide, I want to suggest a sequence of collective patterns that occur in at least certain forms of genocide. At the heart of the task is the question: Why all? What is the source of the impulse to destroy a human group in its entirety?

Otto Rank, the early follower of Freud and subsequent dissident, is a key figure here as a major source of the paradigm of death and the continuity of life—or the symbolization of life and death—that I have been employing here and in other work over several decades. A central tenet of that model is that human beings kill in order to assert their own life-power. To that tenet may now be added the image of curing a deadly disease, so that genocide may become an absolute form of killing in the name of healing. The model I propose includes a perception of collective illness, a vision of a cure, and a series of motivations, experiences, and requirements of perpetrators in their quest for that cure.

The perceived illness is a collectively experienced inundation in death imagery, a shared sense of Kierkegaard's "sickness unto death." It is the despairing edge of historical (or psychohistorical) dislocation, of the breakdown of the symbolic forms and sources of meaning previously shared by a particular human group. That collective sense of immersion in death, bodily and spiritually, could not have been greater than that experienced in Germany after the First World War. But the larger dislocation had begun much earlier. The German struggle with what has been called anti-modern despair goes back at least to the last half of the nineteenth century— so much so that Fritz Stern called his 1961 study of pre-Hitler Germanic ideology *The Politics of Cultural Despair*.

Post–First World War confusion, the experience of the Weimar Republic as "an era of dissolution, without guidance," was at least in part a continuation of that earlier process. By then German culture had begun to divide itself into two camps: the artistic and social experimentalists who tried out every variety of newness in a great rush of creativity and excess; and the right-wing political restorationists who "despised . . . precisely this free-floating spirit of experimentation." Both camps were dealing with an intense experience of loss. There was a breakdown in the symbolization of cultural continuity or of collective immortality.

But the First World War holds the key to the German perception of collective historical illness that was prominent before and during the Nazi regime. For in that experience we find not only death immersion on an extraordinary scale but a survivor experience so intense as to be difficult to grasp even now. The First World War for Germany represented still another crucial psychological dimension, the profound experience of failed regeneration.

The outbreak of the war was marked by exultation or "war fever" among most of the belligerents. For Germany the situation was especially transcendent, so that "regardless of social station or political conviction, August 1914 was a sacred experience." With the defeat, however, adult Germans became the most devastated survivors: of the killing and dying on an unprecedented scale, and of the equally traumatic death of national and social visions, of meaning itself.

This was exemplified by Hitler's own survivor sequence. His subsequent vision and social action can be understood as an effort to re-create "that awesome moment [at the beginning of the First World War] to cleanse it of all impurities." The "disease" with which the Nazis were attempting to cope was death itself, death made unmanageable by "the modern necrophilia" of the First World War, and Hitler, as prophet and savior, came to represent the martyred German dead and serve as their link with the new community of the living.

The sense of historical illness includes a collective hunger for a "cure." If you are curing a sickness, *anything* is permissible. Whatever vision is to qualify as a cure must hold out the promise of shared vitality and renewed confidence in collective immortality. In the twentieth century, any such vision is likely to be bound up with a sense of nation, with what we call "nationalism."

To move in a genocidal direction, that cure must be total. The totalized modern state always claims a higher principle—in this case, purification of the world's most valuable race as a means of curing the prevailing human illness. Totalism in a nation-state, then, is most likely to emerge as a cure for a death-haunted "illness"; and victimization, violence, and genocide are potential aspects of that cure.

Part of the cure is the experience of transcendence: of a psychic state so intense that time and death disappear. The cure must maintain, or at least evoke periodically, that psychic experience. One's own sense of transcendence merges with the image of the endless life of one's people. In that experience—or promise—of ecstasy, one may be ready to kill, or at least to sanction killing.

Hitler became an agent of this transcendence, because of both his oratorical-demagogic genius and the German hunger for transcendence. As he invoked principles of " 'honor,' 'fatherland,' *'Volk,'* 'loyalty,' and 'sacrifice,' his German hearers not only took his words in deadly earnest but hung on them as upon the message of a savior."

Genocide is a response to collective fear of pollution and defilement. It depends upon an impulse toward purification. And the purification and sacrifice are absolute. Hitler had always totalized the genocidal cure: either the Aryan or the Jewish race would be destroyed. He told Albert Speer that, if the war were lost, the German people too were "lost" so one need not worry about their needs for survival. That is, the cure had failed: they had shown themselves weak and unworthy.

At this point, collective suicide (actually the leader taking his people with him in death) had the future-oriented message that the genocidal cure must go on. Hitler's own suicide can be understood as part of the necessity he felt for the entire German people to share a similar sacrificial fate, possibly on behalf of future political resurrection. Just as one reasserts immortalizing principles in killing oneself, so may the self-genocide of the people, mainly engendered by a leader, seek to assert the immortalization of the whole people. That is, the perpetrating individual or the group is cured by self-destruction. Then there can be no danger of hidden infection, of "inner Judaization." Purification and sacrifice are absolute. Self-destruction may well be the *only* logical outcome for those truly committed to genocide.

7
Trump

Donald Trump is a special kind of cultist. He is in no way totalistic—his beliefs can be remarkably fluid—nor is he the leader of a sealed-off cultic community. Rather, his cultism is inseparable from his solipsistic reality. That solipsism emanates only from the self and what the self requires, which makes him the most bizarre and persistent would-be owner of reality. And in his way he has created a community of zealous believers who are geographically dispersed.

A considerable portion of his base can be understood as cultist, as followers of a guru who is teacher, guide, and master. From my studies of cults and cultlike behavior, I recognize this aspect of Trump's relationship to his followers. It is evident at his large-crowd events, which began as campaign rallies but have continued to take place during his presidency. There is a ritual quality to the chants he has led such as "Lock her up!" and "Build that wall!" The latter chant is followed by the guru's question "And who will pay for it?," then the crowd's answer, "Mexico!" The chants and responses are less about policy than they are assertions of guru-disciple ties. The chants are rituals that generate "high states"—or what can even be called experiences of transcendence—in disciples. The back-and-forth brings them closer to the guru and enables them to share his claim to omnipotence and his sacred aura.

Trump does not directly express an apocalyptic narrative, but his presence has an apocalyptic aura. He tells us that, as not only a "genius" but a "very stable genius," he alone can "fix" the terrible problems of our society. To be sure these are bizarre expressions of his extreme grandiosity, but also of a man who would be a savior to a disintegrating world.

Steve Bannon (whether as campaign manager, chief strategist, or outside commentator) has greatly influenced Trump's apocalyptic tendencies in relation to the key American democratic institutions. Bannon tells us that his own goal of "deconstruction of the administrative state" is consistent with Trump's aims as president. He further characterizes Trump's cabinet choices of people opposed to the work of their agencies as consistent with his own wish "to destroy the state." Bannon has served as a facilitator of and a spokesman for the president's state-destroying impulses.

But the most boldly apocalyptic Trump-related expression comes from the bizarrely conspiracist group known as QAnon, which believes Trump is actually working closely with Special Prosecutor Robert Mueller in preventing a coup d'état by Barack Obama, Hillary Clinton, and George Soros. That conspiracy also includes an international child sex-trafficking ring (as derived from an earlier "Pizzagate" conspiracy theory) run by politicians and liberal Hollywood actors. QAnon also uses such apocalyptic names for itself as "The Storm" and "The Great Awakening," both of which refer to a moment of decisive military action in which anti-Trump figures will be incarcerated, including various Democrats Robert Mueller has been secretly investigating.

We may understand this as a version of conspiratorial apocalypse that will enable Trump as a true savior to preside over a politically and morally cleansed world. Trump has not publicly embraced this bizarre group, but adherents wearing QAnon buttons have been appearing at his rallies since the summer of 2018, and a major QAnon promoter was given a photo op in the Oval Office of August of that year. What we can say is that Trump would be very capable of embracing at least a part of the wild QAnon conspiratorial thinking should it contribute to a needed sense of self.

Over the course of his presidency, Trump has become still more grandiose. His lies and falsehoods have not only increased significantly in number but have been more and more in direct violation of concrete evidence in the form of his own recorded statements and tweets. That is, he has gone further than before in asserting an insistent solipsism that defies the most basic and immediate forms of reality. He has also become increasingly agitated, his monologues longer and even looser than before, and has had more difficulty in calling upon the "narrative necessity" to render his lies true.

Above all, Trump's cultist interactions with his base have created an insoluble problem in connection with what is now simply called "the wall." The wall is a messianic promise, and there is deep confusion in both Trump and his followers between the physical entity (a barrier between Mexico and the United States that will never be built) and the metaphysical vision of safety and racial purity.

A dangerous direction on the part of Trump is to translate his falsehoods into policies, as in his sending troops to the border to confront what he declared to be a murderous band of criminals and terrorists who are "invading" our country; in fact the caravan in question was made up mostly of desperate asylum seekers, a large number of them women and children. But the process has to be ultimately self-defeating. The very extension of solipsistic reality to national institutional practice comes to expose its falsehoods and dangers.

The whole process contributes to an expanding sense of Trump's unfitness, affirmed by the writings of psychological professionals. That sense is often shared by Trump's Republican supporters who speak in whispers about his "craziness" while defending him publicly for what they take to be political necessity. The arrangement is ultimately unstable but plays out a dynamic of enormous harm. Remaining followers can take on a Trump-centered identity that is difficult to either sustain or shed.

Overall, the revelations and investigations of Trump's Russian activities, obstructions of justice, and financial illegalities have left him behaving like a man who knows he is in his endgame. To be sure, his extraordinary survivor skills—along with truth-suppressing interventions by such facilitators as Attorney General William Barr— may well enable him to hang in and run for reelection. But it is also possible that he will be forced out of office and contrive a new narrative of victory that includes his brilliant contributions as a savior of our country despite the resistance of his enemies, who can now step down and revive the world's economy by means of his transcendent economic skills.

Donald Trump: "The Assault on Reality"
First published in 2018

An important way to understand Trump and Trumpism is as an assault on reality. At issue is the attempt to control, to own, immediate truth along with any part of history that feeds such truth. Since this behavior stems from Trump's own mind, it is generally attributed to his narcissism (and he has plenty of that). But I would suggest that the more appropriate term is "solipsistic reality." Narcissism suggests self-love and even, in the quaint language of the early psychoanalysts, libido directed at the self. Solipsism has more to do with a cognitive process of interpreting the world exclusively through the experience and needs of the self.

Trump's mindset is the very antithesis of ideological totalism: his ideas readily change and reverse themselves in response to specific situations. Such a relationship to ideas would seem to have nothing to do with ideological totalism. Yet, as different as he is from totalists, he too seeks to control reality.

Trump's solipsism conforms to a tradition in psychology and philosophy for rendering the self an insistent source for all reality. With extreme forms of solipsism the external world and other minds cannot be known and may, in effect, have no existence. What results is continuous falsehood, whether of an almost automatic kind, or of the intentional form we call lying.

Trump's presidency has followed a predictable sequence starting with an initial falsehood (Hillary Clinton's nearly 3 million margin in the popular vote was derived from fraudulent ballots cast mostly by illegal immigrants). As the falsehood radiates outward it becomes increasingly difficult to defend, first on the part of the spokesperson who must turn the falsehood into truth, and still less credible as others examine its claims, until, in its journey through society, it becomes mostly recognized as patent untruth. Yet in the process it not only gets a hearing but lingers as something whose truth—or untruth—is repeatedly examined. To that extent, each of Trump's expressions of solipsistic reality somehow remains "out there." More than that, these falsehoods and lies may be ignored if not embraced by immediate followers who identify passionately with Trump himself, or by Republicans insistent upon holding on to Trump-centered power.

If Trump has no consistent ideology—lacking the conviction and discipline of a fascist or even a populist—he does have a narrative. And that turns out to be important. The narrative does have consistency: America has been great in the past, but has been in the wrong hands and allowed to become weak and misused by foreign forces, especially allies, who cheat and take advantage of us. He, Trump, and only he, has both the strength and negotiating skills to "make America great again." As a strongman and a dealmaker, he will restore America to its rightful world-dominating military and economic power. At the same time his solipsistic self-presentation includes claims to decency, loyalty, and lovability, along with a toughness that will destroy any who treat him unjustly, which means any who call out his lies or falsehoods or in some way oppose him.

The psychologist Jerome Bruner wrote of the narrative construction of reality and pointed out that falsehoods can embody a "narrative necessity" required for the flow and consistency of a larger, encompassing story. The narrative necessity can be crude indeed, given the flagrant untruths of Trump's solipsistic reality. But those untruths can be subsumed to what is claimed to be a larger truth. And when the solipsist holds a position of power he can transform the falsehood into public policy. That was what Trump did when he created a special electoral commission to expose the "fraudulence" of Clinton's popular vote, a commission whose purpose seemed to be that of exercising further control over the electoral process, and which in any case did not last very long.

Yet we should avoid falling into a cult of solipsistic personality. Trump's falsehoods connect with longstanding American Nativist and Know-Nothing movements, and with totalistic contemporary Republican assertions. He in fact draws upon the voices of right-wing extremism, what Todd Gitlin calls "The Vortex" of "the Birthers, Whitewater, 'Travelgate,' and Vince Foster conspiracy theorists, 'death panel' enthusiasts, 'Lock her up!' chanters, scientist-haters and other Flat Earth factions." In other words Trump's solipsism can connect with a sea of mostly right-wing exaggeration, misinformation, conspiracism, falsehood, and lies.

Is Trump's solipsism, then, simply an extension of a cultural trend in American life? I would argue that it is something more. Despotic control over reality usually relates to specific goals, those having to do with the dictator's holding onto power or furthering his pet projects. Trump is different. His solipsism is sui generis. He is psychologically remarkable in his capacity to manufacture and continuously assert falsehood in the apparent absence of psychosis. Those suffering from schizophrenic psychosis, for instance, can also be highly solipsistic in their hallucinations and delusions. But Trump does not appear to have hallucinations or delusions in a structured, classical sense. That is, without being psychotic, he is just as solipsistic as those who are. He in fact manifests a considerable talent for manipulating his solipsistic falsehoods in ways that enhance his own narrative and connect with related political projects.

In that sense Trump has an extraordinary psychological capacity for sustained solipsism. Have we ever encountered a public figure who has so consistently reversed truth and falsehood and done so on so such a vast scale? David Leonhardt, the journalist who has probably done the most to track Trump's lies, describes him (with co-writers) as "virtually indifferent to reality, often saying whatever helps him make the case he's trying to make," and as "trying to make truth irrelevant." It is difficult to overestimate the dangers that stem from such extreme assaults on reality by a man who holds the most powerful office in the world.

Does Trump believe his own falsehoods? The question itself suggests a clear dichotomy between belief and disbelief, which is not always the way things work. In studying people's behavior under extremity, I have found that the mind can simultaneously believe and not believe in something, and can move in and out of belief according to perceived pressures. I could witness that tendency in false confessions made by European missionaries accused of being spies and subjected to brutal versions of thought reform in Chinese prisons. One priest told me how, after experiencing unbearable pain from torture, he came to imagine a "spy radio" in his mission house and to view talks he had with other priests about the approaching Communist army as a form of "espionage" on behalf of the "imperialists." He spoke of it as similar to writing a novel in which events in the novel become understood as actual history. Trump has been subjected to no such external abuse, but his own inner conflicts and anxieties could create his own version of abuse. The larger point is that, like all other forms of human behavior, belief can be a form of adaptation to existing conditions.

Consider Trump's most egregiously self-serving lie: that Barack Obama was not born in this country and therefore an illegitimate president. Trump did not invent that lie but embraced it and became one of its most persistent articulators. Consciously and repeatedly, he manipulated the lie as a way to enter presidential politics. But to make one's falsehoods convincing one has to develop a belief in them, and it is likely that in some part of his mind Trump has believed (and may still believe) in Obama's foreign birth. The larger narrative of illegitimacy and racism becomes crucial in providing a structured story that can encompass the falsehood and allow for its further manipulation.

But this "narrative necessity" can itself be unstable. Trump's solipsism will likely destroy his presidency. Yet along the way something is happening to the rest of us as well. We are experiencing what can be called "reality fatigue." The drumbeat of falsehoods and lies continues even as we expose them as such: we are thrust into a realm in which a major segment of our society ignores or defies the principles of reason, evidence, and shared knowledge that are required for the function of a democracy. But some of these seemingly unquestioning followers may come to experience conflict over this unreal reality.

The Messianic Wall and the Ultra-Loyal Base
First published in 2019

There is much talk of Trump's ultra-loyal political base, and rightly so. That base, or at least the most passionate element of it, consists of angry people who feel spurned by the political establishment. The base showed its psychological and political clout when Rush Limbaugh and Ann Coulter, who claimed to speak for it, denounced Trump for "caving" to a unanimous Senate decision to keep the government running, which caused Trump to reverse himself and create a disastrous partial government shutdown.

Yet that same base could play a large part in removing Trump from office. People who submit themselves to an omnipotent guru can be especially passionate in their support of all that he says and does. But this cultism can also be a source of vulnerability for both. Leaders and followers can become antagonists rather than mutual nurturers.

Consider the chants about erecting the wall and Mexico paying for it. There is widespread skepticism about the wall ever being built. Lindsey Graham made that inference when he spoke of the wall as a "metaphor" for Trump's policies. But it is much more than that, something close to a messianic promise—one of absolute "safety" and, in a sense, national purity. The wall and its chants sustain both a political dynamic, Trump's strength in not "caving" to his enemies, and a cultic dynamic—the merger of master and follower.

Inevitably there is confusion between the messianic vision and the concrete or steel structure. That confusion is experienced by Trump's followers and undoubtedly in considerable measure by Trump himself. The question then arises whether Trump's power as a political leader and as a cultic leader has come to depend upon producing an actual wall. And whether this issue has already begun to raise doubts in the minds of some of his followers.

Trump has been observed to be "afraid of his base," a fear usually attributed to his need for their support as his best means of avoiding impeachment. But the fear may also spring from the contradiction between messianic vision and physical structure. Since early 2019, the number of rallies has tapered off, which suggests that Trump senses that they no longer do quite as much for him or his followers as they have in the past.

Much is at stake here. Many of Trump's followers have offered themselves to him with confidence that he will continue to provide them with a true path. When he falters and can no longer serve these needs, his followers may not only feel deprived but angered by a sense of betrayal. The chants and especially the promise of the wall may lose their power as he is unable to convey convincingly either the metaphysical or physical aspect of the wall. Followers may become frustrated and angry, even to the point of denouncing the worshiped guru. And Trump himself, who needs his followers as much as they need him, may also experience stress to the point of psychological breakdown.

I observed that sequence in my study of the fanatical Japanese cult, Aum Shinrikyō. When its guru Shōkō Asahara was imprisoned and put on trial, he was divested of his status as a guru. Disciples who had venerated him and had shared "mystical experiences" were quick to testify against him and reveal details of his deceptions and crimes. One such disciple, perhaps his closest, described Asahara's full role in directing the sarin attack and denounced him as a "false guru." Another told of being "deceived" by the guru, and declared that Asahara's boast of achieving "final liberation" and other claims were "complete nonsense," made by a "foolish human being." Significantly, in the midst of these accusations, Asahara himself lapsed into psychosis. What had previously been what I called a "functional megalomania" was no longer functional.

Trump's situation with his followers is very different from that of Asahara and Aum Shinrikyō. Trump has had no clear-cut cultic community within which he has lived as guru. But he did create a dispersed community of fanatical followers who see him as a political and prophetic master. Should many of these followers view him as no longer able to satisfy their needs—whether because of confusions having to do with the wall or other actions causing them economic or social pain—they too could turn against him.

Of course, the withdrawal of support from Trump by

Republicans in Congress is crucial to bringing about the end to his presidency. These Republicans were never his disciples so much as his political allies or, as it has turned out, his political pawns.

But we should not lose sight of the potentially changeable passions of those who make up Trump's base, especially passions with cultic components. At the point where Trump can no longer satisfy a significant number of these followers—a point we may be approaching—the fierceness of their earlier support can be quickly transformed into the anger of the betrayed. When that happens, the previously "safe" base becomes the greatest threat to Trump's presidency.

Social Media

During the Trump presidency, the internet has itself become a purveyor of claimed reality. Any group—indeed, any individual person—can make use of the internet to disseminate the most bizarre version of ultimate reality, and can do so anonymously.

I have mentioned QAnon as a largely social media–created apocalyptic conspiracy theory. Another internet product is the "Cult of Kek," the alt-right's semi-ironic religion, which claims the reappearance of Kek, the mythological Egyptian God of Chaos and Darkness, sometimes taking the form of Pepe the Frog. In this narrative, Donald Trump has become the embodiment of this Kek/Pepe chaos, the prophet of the world-destruction sought by the alt-right.

Conspiracies abound not only from professional conspiracists such as *Alex Jones and his website and radio show* InfoWars, *but on many different websites and "imageboards," such as 4chan, 8chan, and Reddit, that are part of the "dark media" where rules need not apply. Twitter itself plays an enormous role as both hub and disseminator of conspiracism.*

A still more sobering social media example of a different kind, one so important that it could well have influenced the presidential election of 2016, was the cooperation between Cambridge Analytica and Facebook. Cambridge Analytica, a political data firm, was largely the creation of Steve Bannon and his billionaire sponsor, Robert Mercer. One former co-executive referred to Cambridge Analytica as "Bannon's arsenal of weaponry to wage a culture war on America using military strategies."

Cambridge Analytica combined a particularly vicious version of traditional "dirty tricks" with cutting-edge social media savvy. The dirty tricks, according to its former CEO, Alexander Nix, included bribery, sting operations, the use of prostitutes, and "honey traps" (usually involving sexual behavior, sometimes even initiated for the purposes of obtaining compromising photographs) to discredit politicians on whom it conducted opposition research.

The social media savvy included advanced methods developed by the Psychometrics Centre of Cambridge University. Aleksandr Kogan, a young Russian American psychologist working there, created an app that enabled him to gain access to elaborate private information on more than fifty million Facebook users, information specifically identifying personality traits that influenced behavior. Kogan had strong links to Facebook, which failed to block his harvesting of that massive data; he then passed the data along to Cambridge Analytica. Kogan also taught at the Saint Petersburg State University in Russia; and given the links between Cambridge Analytica and Russian groups, the material was undoubtedly made available to Russian intelligence. So extensive was Cambridge Analytica's collection of data that Nix could boast, "Today in the United States we have somewhere close to 4 or 5 thousand data points on every individual. . . . So we model the personality of every adult across the United States, some 230 million people." Whatever his exaggeration, he was describing a new means of milieu control that was invisible and potentially manipulable in the extreme.

Beyond Cambridge Analytica or Kogan, Russian penetration of American social media has come to be recognized as a vast enterprise involving extensive falsification and across-the-board anti-Clinton messages, with special attention given to African American men in order to discourage them from voting. The Russians apparently reached millions of people and surely had a considerable influence on the outcome of the election. More generally, one can say that social media platforms can now create a totality of their own, and can make themselves available to would-be owners of reality by means of massive deception, distortion, and promulgation of falsehoods. The technology itself promotes mystification and becomes central to creating and sustaining cultism.

Trump is the first president to have available to him these developments in social media. His stance toward the wild conspiracism I have mentioned is to stop short of total allegiance to *them, but at the same time to facilitate them and call them forth in his tweets and harbor their followers at his rallies.*

All of this suggests not only that Trump and the new social media are made for each other, but also that the problem will long outlive Trump's brief, but all too long, moment on the historical stage.

8

The Apocalyptic Twins:
Nuclear and Climate Threats

I have not included excerpts on nuclear and climate threats, each of which could destroy our civilization. But I want to say more about these "apocalyptic twins" and their specific relation to cultism.

I have mentioned the phenomenon of nuclearism as a worshipful attitude toward doomsday weapons. The phenomenon includes a perverse—I would say cultist—spiritualization of the weapons that has endowed them with the capacity to purify the human mind.

That expression of nuclearism began even before bombs were dropped on Hiroshima and Nagasaki. It occurred at Los Alamos, New Mexico, where the bombs were created, in a series of conversations between two gifted and humanistic scientists, Niels Bohr and Robert Oppenheimer. Bohr, the deeply revered Danish mentor of Oppenheimer and many others, developed the concept of "complementarity"—the idea that two very different findings in physics can be equally true. For instance, matter could be accurately represented by particles or by waves. In their reflections the two men came to believe that they could apply this principle to the atomic bomb: if used, it would bring out a new dimension of destruction but would also create an equally new dedication to peace. As Richard Rhodes put it, "The bomb for Bohr and Oppenheimer was a weapon of death that might also end war and redeem mankind." For these two extraordinary minds to come to this strange syllogism suggests the great temptation, from the beginning, to associate the bomb with spiritual enlightenment.

Bohr and Oppenheimer could be viewed as early members, perhaps the creators, of the nuclear priesthood. As with any priesthood, views could vary within it, and even in the same mind. Bohr and Oppenheimer, for instance, were early advocates of finding ways to share nuclear secrets with other nations; Oppenheimer strongly favored the use of the first atomic bomb—"his" bomb—but would later become a leading spokesman for opposition to the larger hydrogen bombs. The nuclear priesthood expanded into a large array of "defense intellectuals" who used their arcane knowledge to project equally arcane scenarios of fighting and surviving and winning nuclear wars. There have been moments of rebellion and outrage on the part of the general population, as in the powerful anti-nuclear expressions of the early 1980s. But on the whole, nuclear weapons have been hard to incorporate into a democratic process. Ordinary people have had difficulty grasping either the science of the weapons or their world-ending potential. The result has been widespread psychic numbing, which in turn has led to greater authority and power on the part of the nuclear priesthood.

The testing of the weapons has always been experimental in seeking to learn their effects on human beings as well as on the overall human habitat. Even the bombs dropped on Hiroshima and Nagasaki had much to do with probing their impact on densely populated urban areas. The lessons one drew from these explorations could vary.

For me that lesson was to be found in the phrase I have used, one plane, one bomb, one city, suggesting an accompanying urgency either to eliminate or bring strong control over the weapons. But there could also be an opposite conclusion to the use of the bomb on these two cities. For the physicist and nuclear strategist Edward Teller, the "Legacy of Hiroshima" was the nuclearistic insistence on building more and better bombs in a constant struggle to sustain an advantage over all of one's adversaries—because "if we stop, we are falling behind." Teller went on to promote these doomsday weapons, explaining that their stockpiling and our readiness to use them were expressions of national courage, since (and, trying to sound like Franklin D. Roosevelt) only our fear of doom was likely to "defeat us." Here we may speak of the cult of nuclearism.

We can say the same of the "logical" discussions and policies about the "modernization" of nuclear weapons. The word modernization suggests removing the rust from aging structures to keep them functioning properly, and there is talk about "renovation," "refurbishment," or "rebuilding," but what modernization largely amounts to is modifying the weapons to make them more usable than the large hydrogen bombs. That entails technologies for diminished explosive power as a form of miniaturization, which can produce Hiroshima-sized nuclear devices that blur distinctions between nuclear and "conventional" weapons. There lies the madness of the logic of modernization.

The elaborate structure of men and weaponry could at times seem to take on a mind of its own. As one observer put it, "In a sense the system built itself and only the system knows how it would respond to insult." And another: "The button is set so finely it could push itself." Here we encounter an early expression of the extreme danger that our technical-robotic creations become the decision makers that bring about near-apocalyptic destruction, whether these "decision-makers" are drones or other forms of sophisticatedly programed weaponry. This sense of techno-bureaucratic mysticism enables people to be all too ready to turn the whole issue over to the nuclear priesthood. That attitude blinds us to the importance of human decisions, or failure to make them, in bringing about this danger. And while the members of the nuclear priesthood can at times express nuclear truths, the priesthood itself tends to be dominated by dangerous versions of nuclearism.

We need to recognize the inherent apocalypticism of these weapons, as revealed in Mao Zedong's vision of a nuclear war resulting in "a truly beautiful future."

Climate Cultism

Our image of climate change moves back and forth between incremental and apocalyptic dangers. Given the extreme climate events to which we have recently been afflicted, the tendency is toward imagery of the apocalyptic. People who resist climate truths can no longer be seen as simple deniers. Because they inevitably know in some part of their minds that climate change is real, they are better termed "climate rejecters," unable to take in or act upon global warming because of their existing worldview, identity, or political affiliations. They are particularly likely to question the human contribution to climate, and readily move toward a biblical view that a dramatic change in the climate could only be an act of God. They are influenced by such biblical events as the Great Flood that brought about Noah's Ark as God's punishment for disobeying his laws. With the dramatic recent increase in the recognition of global warming, the rejecters have come to constitute a narrowing community of falsehood. In that way they resemble the Flat Earth Cult, which still has members who also refer to what they believe to be a biblical claim.

Significantly, climate rejecters often accuse scientific truth-tellers of constituting a "doomsday cult," which could be partially a form of psychological projection but also an expression of repressed awareness of their own relation to a potential doomsday. In any case, climate change rejecters are likely to become an increasingly beleaguered group involving cultist gurus and followers.

There could appear other end-time climate cults, possibly

looking to the biblical model of Noah's Ark. Some of these cults could come to see world destruction as a necessary prelude to purification. A few could even embrace a version of "forcing the end": joining in some form of apocalyptic narrative in order to hasten renewal and purification. Or they could seek to fend off doomsday, or slow it down, in favor of their own teachings. Climate cults could express impulses we are unable at this time to predict. What I call the climate swerve—the greater recognition of global warming—is on the whole a hopeful human development. But it could at the same time stimulate destructive cultist behavior in the service of increasingly desperate rejection of climate truths.

Climate truths, moreover, can bring about despair in climate activists to the extent of taking them to psychological terrain that may border on cultism. I have in mind the often admirable but troubling trajectory of the Dark Mountain Project, which is based mainly in England but also operates in other parts of the world. Paul Kingsnorth, its leader, tells us of his recognition that his and others' climate activism was built on false hope since global warming, in his view, will inevitably destroy us in our "age of ecocide"; and of his "joyous" abandonment of that hope in favor of a commitment to "uncivilization." The Dark Mountain Project has centered on probing the sources of our lethal civilization and has produced a series of respected books by concerned writers and artists.

But Kingsnorth admitted to an interviewer that he has ambivalence about whether he even wants civilization to survive, given what he considers to be the essential harm that would be done by the technology that would be invoked, whether in stemming global warming or building the wind farms and solar devices of renewable energy.

A *New York Times* reporter told how, in 2013, at a Dark Mountain Project festival, there was a ritual of masked figures kneeling at the base of a sculptured tree and a ceremonial burning of that sculpture at midnight with an accompanying chant: "We are gathered. We are gathered. We are gathered." After that people "danced, sang, laughed, barked, growled, hooted, mooed, bleated, and meowed, forming a kind of atavistic improvisatory choir." While the Dark Mountain Project has in recent years focused more on books than on festivals, the midnight ritual suggests that it or related groups could take their preoccupation with nature and non-human animals in a cultic direction, celebrating the demise of our species.

More generally, one wonders at the broad psychological fear regarding an apocalypse over which we feel we have no control. Even with nuclear weapons, we sense that we can make decisions over whether we build or use them. With climate, there can be the feeling among many that nothing we do will help, that we are doomed by events we have no capacity to influence. All this is an example—the ultimate example—of the role activism can play both in mitigating extreme danger and overcoming collective despair.

Part Three

Regaining Reality

9

The Protean Alternative

I have stressed the pervasiveness and danger of cultism, but that does not mean it must dominate our future. We are capable of alternatives—even antidotes—that stem from the very structure of the human mind. One such alternative is what I call the protean self, a view of the self as always in process; as being many-sided rather than monolithic, and resilient rather than fixed.

The protean self is a way of adapting to significant historical dislocation and change. It is at the same time an expression of the basic human need for symbolization. This need extends further than the Freudian view of symbols: of one image representing another, such as "stick" or "umbrella" equals "penis," and "cave" or "suitcase" equals "vagina." Rather, I draw upon the twentieth-century philosophical principle of "symbolic forms" or "symbolic transformations" as put forward by Ernst Cassirer and Susanne K. Langer. According to this tradition, we human beings perceive nothing nakedly but must reconstruct every perception on the basis of the mind's previous experience. That is, we have no choice but to make everything new. Cassirer thus speaks of human beings as the "animal symbolicum." And Langer refers to "the transformational nature of human nature," and to "the mind's symbol-making function [as] one of man's primary activities, like eating, looking or moving about . . . the essential act of mind." Both suggest that the mind is biologically grounded in our symbolizing function. That function is now known to be primarily located in the large and uniquely influential human forebrain. We have seen how this symbolizing function can take us to dangerous places: for example, Nazi racial theory and biomedical vision, and Aum Shinrikyō's apocalyptic narrative requiring the cult to join in "forcing the end." But that same symbolizing function is also a profound evolutionary achievement, providing a capacity for imagination that is largely responsible for the genius of human adaptation.

In my work I have seen this characteristic of the self—what I would now call an engine of symbolization—as an antidote to the destructive projects I have studied. At the end of my book on the coercive process of thought reform, I wrote a chapter on antithetical expressions of "open personal change." In my work on Hiroshima, I described how some exposed to the bomb could take on a "survivor mission," which enabled them to transform their sense of self from passive victim to active witness and to travel around the world telling their stories. In my research on anti-war Vietnam veterans, I found that they could undergo significant change in worldview and in sense of self much more quickly than our prior psychological views about adult change would allow; and they could experience what I called "animating guilt" by converting self-condemnation into the anxiety of responsibility in their public opposition to the war. Even in my work with Auschwitz survivors I encountered prisoner doctors *(mostly Jewish, but also non-Jewish Poles and Germans) who, when given an opportunity to provide minimal medical care, managed to remain genuine healers.*

More generally, we seem to be wired for the potential expression of either proteanism or cultism. Cultism, in fact, is largely a reaction to protean multiplicity and the anxieties it produces in connection with the loss of a sense of certainty. Cultism narrows the symbolizing function of the self to the model offered by political totalism or guru-centered reality claims. In this way, cultism interferes with the profound connection between self and history. Proteanism, in contrast, seeks to restore the self's broader symbolizing function and its overall connection to the historical process.

Proteanism, though offering no guarantees about the human future, can help us to stem the cultist loss of reality and reassert an openness to the world.

Protean Self
First published in 1993

We are becoming fluid and many-sided. Without quite realizing it, we have been evolving a sense of self appropriate to the restlessness and flux of our time. This mode of being differs radically from that of the past, and enables us to engage in continuous exploration and personal experiment. I have named it the "protean self" after Proteus, the Greek sea god of many forms.

The protean self emerges from confusion, from the widespread feeling that we are losing our psychological moorings.

We feel ourselves buffeted about by unmanageable historical forces and social uncertainties. Leaders appear suddenly, recede equally rapidly, and are difficult for us to believe in when they are around. We change ideas and partners frequently, and do the same with jobs and places of residence. Enduring moral convictions, clear principles of action and behavior—we believe these must exist, but where? Whether dealing with world problems or child rearing, our behavior tends to be ad hoc, more or less decided upon as we go along. We are beset by a contradiction: we are schooled in the virtues of constancy and stability—whether as individuals, groups, or nations—yet our world and our lives seem inconstant and utterly unpredictable. We readily come to view ourselves as unsteady, neurotic, or worse.

But rather than collapse under these threats and pulls, the self turns out to be surprisingly resilient. It makes use of bits and pieces here and there and somehow keeps going. What may seem to be mere tactical flexibility, or just bungling along, turns out to be much more than that. We find ourselves evolving a self of many possibilities, one that has risks and pitfalls but at the same time holds out considerable promise for the human future.

The protean self did not suddenly appear in full bloom. It emerged from a certain social and historical context. What we call the self—one's inclusive sense (or symbolization) of one's own being—is enormously sensitive to the flow of history. In the case of Chinese and Japanese people I interviewed for different studies, that flow took extreme forms of war and upheaval. While America has undergone no such large-scale twentieth-century disaster, our history has included colonization and revolution, movement toward the western frontier, the carnage of our civil war, massive immigration, participation in at least five major wars outside of our territory during this century, and continuous technological development and social change—all of which have had a formidable influence on the contemporary self. For these historical forces not only manipulate the self from the outside but shape it importantly from within.

Historical influences contributing to the protean self can be traced back to the Enlightenment and even the Renaissance in the West, and to at least the Meiji Restoration of the nineteenth century in Japan. These influences include the dislocations of rapid historical change, the mass media revolution, and the threat of human extinction. All have undergone an extraordinary acceleration during the last half of the twentieth century, causing a radical breakdown of prior communities and sources of authority. At the same time, ways of reconstituting the self in the midst of radical uncertainty have also evolved. So much so that the protean self in our time has become a modus vivendi, a "mode of living." This is especially true in our own country.

The same historical forces can, however, produce an apparently opposite reaction: the closing off of the person and the constriction of self-process. It can take the form of widespread psychic numbing—diminished capacity or inclination to feel—and a general sense of stasis and meaninglessness. Or it can lead to an expression of totalism, of demand for absolute dogma and a monolithic self. A prominent form of totalism in our day is fundamentalism. Broadly understood, fundamentalism includes a literalized doctrine, religious or political, enclosed upon itself by the immutable words of the holy books. The doctrine is rendered both sacred in the name of a past of perfect harmony that never was, and central to a quest for collective revitalization. But the totalistic or fundamentalist response is a reaction to proteanism and to the fear of chaos. While proteanism is able to function in a world of uncertainty and ambiguity, fundamentalism wants to wipe out that world in favor of a claim to definitive truth and unalterable moral certainty. The "death sentence" imposed on the writer Salman Rushdie, an Indian-born Muslim, by Ayatollah Khomeini, the Iranian Muslim imam (or supreme guide), symbolizes painfully the contemporary struggle between proteanism and fundamentalism. Khomeini was reacting to Rushdie's highly irreverent treatment of leading Muslim religious figures in his novel *The Satanic Verses*, depictions that were part of the author's wildly imaginative proteanism and of the novel's central question: "How does newness come into the world?"

In the waning years of the twentieth century, we have witnessed something close to a worldwide epidemic of fundamentalism: religious forms in Christianity, Judaism, Hinduism, and Islam; and political forms in various expressions of extreme nationalism (such as the Serbian attack on other groups and demand for "ethnic cleansing" in what was formerly Yugoslavia) and of neo-Nazi views in Germany and elsewhere. The issue of *control*, of stemming the protean tide, always looms large. Yet the polarization between protean-ism and fundamentalism turns out to be less than absolute. In research interviews, fundamentalists revealed themselves to be frequently confused and ambivalent concerning their own principles, and susceptible to a proteanism of their own. Proteanism and fundamentalism represent, however, a basic historical dynamic that is crucial for this study and for the world in general.

For many years, I have been exploring the dark side of human behavior—Chinese thought reform (or "brainwash-ing"), the Vietnam War, Hiroshima, and, darkest of all, Nazi doctors. I have done so in the hope that, by probing the psy-chology of evil and destructiveness, we would be better able to combat this behavior and seek alternatives. Here, transfor-mation itself becomes my subject. The protean self represents an alternative to violence. Violence always has an absolute quality: behavior is reduced to a single, narrow focus; and in that sense, violence is a dead end. Proteanism, in contrast, provides a capacity to avoid dead ends.

The malleability of the self can even be sustained under despotism, as evidenced by the worldwide movement, during the late 1980s, for freedom and broader human possibili-ties: the democracy movement in China, the overturning of Soviet-dominated Communist states throughout Central and Eastern Europe (Poland, Czechoslovakia, Hungary, East Germany, Romania, Bulgaria, and Albania), and the struggle against apartheid in South Africa.

Individual and collective malleability were also evident both in the shift in Soviet-American relations during the late

1980s, when unrelenting antipathy and mutual nuclear threat turned to shared commitment to reduction of stockpiles and peaceful cooperation; and in the subsequent breakup of the Soviet Union and replacement by a confusing array of independent republics. These radical turnabouts on a collective scale reflected equally radical changes in the mindsets of not only individuals like Mikhail Gorbachev and Boris Yeltsin, of Ronald Reagan and George H. W. Bush, but of legions of decision makers and millions of ordinary people in the former Soviet Union and the United States. There followed in turn the stunning developments in the American presidential election of 1992, including the emergence of a bizarre but formidable third-party movement led by Ross Perot and, most dramatic of all, the victory of a previously unknown political figure, Bill Clinton.

The post-Communist chaos throughout Central and Eastern Europe—its most extreme expression the war and genocidal policies in the former Yugoslavia—reflects darker patterns that can result from large-scale change. Putin's Russia serves as an example here. The same is true of the civil wars and widespread starvation occurring in various parts of Africa. There are also the persisting American national confusions and antagonisms, whether associated with economic duress and unemployment, race, crime and drugs, or major breakdowns in such areas as education and health care. Nor are these national and international antagonisms and breakdowns the last word; rather, they are part of a continuing pattern of upheaval and change.

Of the greatest importance here is the fact that virtually

no one anticipated these developments. In Czechoslovakia, for instance, the successful "revolutionaries" were taken aback by the "surprising quickness of the collapse" of the Communist regime and had to "define and redefine the identity of the state." There are many reasons for that failure to anticipate either the liberating revolutions or the subsequent expressions of chaos, but one of them is surely our underestimation of the self's capacity for shifts and reversals. With that recognition, we now sense that human history has become increasingly open, dangerous, and unpredictable. It has also become more visible to people everywhere, as the mass media—notably the social media—bombard us with history's tragedies and achievements. In the headlines of any given day we encounter a dizzying array of twentieth-century fragmentations, deformations, and human struggles. No place on the globe is immune from them.

Over decades of observation, I have come to see that the older version of personal identity, at least insofar as it suggests inner stability and sameness, was derived from a vision of a traditional culture in which relationships to symbols and institutions are still relatively intact—hardly the case in the last years of the twentieth century or the first two decades of the twenty first. If the self is a symbol of one's organism, the protean self-process is the continuous psychic re-creation of that symbol. Although the process is by no means without confusion and danger, it allows for an opening out of individual life, for a self of many possibilities.

One seeks lasting human ties and sustained ethical

commitments; although these, too, can be uncertain and susceptible to their own shifts, they can also be subject to various kinds of renewal. Indeed, a large question for the protean self, and one that cannot be answered simply, concerns its capacity to sustain and live out moral principles in the midst of psychological flux. For the entire life cycle, no longer governed by formal rites of passage, tends to be subject to considerable improvisation. The protean self tends also to be aware of historical process and of planetary connections, but is uncertain how to understand and act on that awareness. The overall quest involves a struggle for larger human connectedness, for ways of symbolizing immortality in the form of attachments that transcend one's limited life span.

Much that I say here about multiplicity is consistent with contemporary cultural and intellectual expressions now designated as "postmodern." As early as the late 1960s, I had used that adjective in connection with proteanism. However convoluted the term has since become, it is meant to suggest a significant late twentieth-century break, or at least a transition, from what is called the "project of modernity"—equally hard to define but seen as taking shape from the Enlightenment of the eighteenth century and including various forms of liberating knowledge and experience, along with confining expressions of rationalism, sweeping ideological claim, and technicism. In fact, tendencies toward multiplicity to the point of fragmentation are rampant in both the modern and the postmodern, but the latter embraces these tendencies—"swims, even wallows, in the fragmentary and the chaotic currents of change." In that sense, proteanism is consistent with what is called the "contingency, multiplicity, and polyvocality" of postmodernism in the arts and with its "playful, self-ironizing" patterns. Because postmodernism has taken on a vast and many-sided theoretical structure of its own, I shall use the word sparingly and attempt to focus my observations and interpretations on how people behave, experience themselves psychologically, and express themselves imaginatively.

I must separate myself, however, from those observers, postmodern or otherwise, who equate multiplicity and fluidity with disappearance of the self, with a complete absence of coherence among its various elements. I would claim the opposite: proteanism involves a quest for authenticity and meaning, a form-seeking assertion of self. The recognition of complexity and ambiguity may well represent a certain maturation in our concept of self. The protean self seeks to be both fluid and grounded, however tenuous that combination. There is nothing automatic about the enterprise, no "greening of the self," but rather a continuous effort without clear termination. Proteanism, then, is a balancing act between responsive shape-shifting, on the one hand, and efforts to consolidate and cohere on the other.

Proteanism involves choice. My conviction is that certain manifestations of proteanism are not only desirable but necessary for the human future. For proteanism can provide a path for the species. That is, proteanism presses toward human commonality, as opposed to the fixed and absolute moral and psychological divisions favored by fundamentalism. In that sense, Khomeini's condemnation of Rushdie was a fundamentalist attack not only on proteanism but on species consciousness. For there is a trajectory, never automatic but always possible, from the protean self to the species self—to the formation of a sense of self based significantly upon one's connection to humankind. Here as elsewhere, proteanism provides no panacea for grave human problems. What it does offer is a potential for change and renewal, for tapping human resiliency. In any case, proteanism is integral to our historical situation, to our contemporary fate.

10

Regaining Reality

In recent work I have referred to "malignant normality," by which I mean the imposition of a norm of destructive or violent behavior, so that such behavior is expected or required of people. I came to this idea through my study of Nazi doctors. The physicians arriving at Auschwitz were expected to carry out selections of Jews for the gas chambers. That was their job. Whatever conflicts they experienced, the great majority adapted to that malignant normality.

With Trump and Trumpism, we have had no such murderous arrangement in American society, but we have experienced a national malignant normality of our own: extensive lying and falsification, systemic corruption, ad hominem attacks on critics, dismissal of intelligence institutions and findings, rejection of climate change truths and of scientists who express them, rebukes of our closest international allies and embrace of dictators, and scornful delegitimization of the party of opposition. This constellation of malignant normality has threatened, and at times virtually replaced, American democracy.

As citizens, and especially as professionals, we need to bear witness to malignant normality and expose it. We then become what I call "witnessing professionals," who draw upon their knowledge and experience to reveal the danger of that malignant normality and actively oppose it. That inevitably includes entering into social and political struggles against expressions of malignant normality.

We have a historical model for combating malignant normality in which the protean self can combine with what Václav Havel, the Czech writer and revolutionary, called "living in truth." Havel's Velvet Revolution against Communist suppression took place in Czechoslovakia in 1989, and there were similar successful uprisings in other Eastern European countries. As Havel explained, "If the main pillar of the system is living a lie, then it is not surprising that the main fundamental threat to it is living the truth." That was not easy under a regime depending on falsehoods for its claimed legitimacy. But Havel spoke of "parallel structures" that formed a "second culture" separate from and antithetical to the regime. He helped create an expanding community of people who lived in freedom, who lived as though there was no oppressive regime controlling their lives. He could then find opposition to the regime "at the level of human consciousness and conscience, the existential level," and could speak of (as in the title of his classic essay) "The Power of the Powerless."

I was able to visit Prague ten months after the successful revolution and to speak to a number of people close to Havel who described their own experiences in carrying out his principles. They found that they could call upon aspects of their selves that they didn't know existed: a ne'er-do-well part-time musician became a completely reliable organizer and distributor of an important underground newsletter. A writer denied publishing outlets by the regime came to work effectively with mental patients and then became an adviser to the president of the new democracy. What I called "Proteus in Prague" was the capacity of individual people for attitudes, actions, and skills they had not previously recognized in themselves.

I also realized that I had earlier encountered that kind of community, not in Czechoslovakia but in Poland. There, in 1978 and 1979, I was able to experience a "second culture" in action when I worked together with members of the Department of Psychiatry at the University Medical Center in Krakow. Psychiatric colleagues there contributed greatly to the interviews I did with Polish survivors of Auschwitz, providing me with help of every kind and with valuable counsel. I was struck by how open and candid they were with me and with each other in their wide-ranging observations about everything from Auschwitz and its survivors, to the practice of psychiatry in Poland, to the Communist regime whose power they were all too well aware of even as they refused to allow it to control their lives or distort their truths.

No wonder that Mohandas Gandhi spoke similarly of his nonviolent resistance as "experiments with truth," and Erik Erikson used the title *Gandhi's Truth* for his psychobiographical study of the Mahatma. Or that Henry David Thoreau, whom Gandhi read, declared, "Rather than love, than money, than fame, give me truth." Havel, Gandhi, and Thoreau sought to live out humane truths that challenged the falsehoods imposed upon them by what they perceived as the malignant normality of their societies. They demonstrated how truth-telling can connect with other forms of life-enhancing activism that are at the heart of opposition to solipsistic falsehoods of any kind. The fragility of such truth-telling movements is all too evident in the recent reemergence of repressive regimes in Eastern Europe and in the vicissitudes of India after Gandhi. But still, those truth-telling movements remain a vital model for us in our unending psychological and political struggles.

For that model to hold we need to recognize the vulnerability of American society to a solipsistic individual like Trump. The loss of reality in American society has a long history and an egregious reactivation in various twentieth-century movements that emphasized conspiracy theories and were summarized by the historian Richard Hofstadter as "The Paranoid Style in American Politics." In combating these assaults on reality we retain the advantage of working institutions that still apply reality-based rather than solipsistic criteria to their investigations, legal decisions, and journalistic probings.

Cultist attacks on those institutions will not go away. But neither will our capacity for openness and truth-telling as alternatives to the closed world of cultism.

Acknowledgments

This book was first suggested by Carl Bromley of The New Press and he maintained his strong support for it as it took on a trajectory of its own. Richard Morris, my agent at Janklow & Nesbit, has contributed much on all levels. Emily Albarillo of The New Press expertly enhanced the book's blending of excerpts from earlier work with new commentaries. Brian Baughan provided manuscript editing that was both imaginative and practical. Discussions with Chuck Strozier and Peter Balakian helped me clarify many of the book's ideas. Jane Isay, my editor for life, once more infused my efforts with her wisdom. Carolyn Mugar provided both research support and great encouragement. Bailey Georges assisted me with everything, and became a close collaborator in her work on excerpts and integration of commentaries. And Nancy Rosenblum brought her remarkable intellect, warmth, and savvy to our continuous conversation about this book and all else.

Notes

Introduction: On the Ownership of Reality

2 Beginning in the late 1970s: Personal communication from the psychologist Steven Hassan, now an authority on cults, who made use of "Chapter 22" in being "deprogrammed" in 1976 from his membership in the Unification Church.

4 Harvey Cox, the venturesome: Harvey Cox, *Turning East: The Promise and the Peril of the New Orientalism* (New York: Simon and Schuster, 1977).

4 Margaret Singer, the talented psychologist: Margaret Thaler Singer, *Cults in Our Midst: The Continuing Fight against Their Hidden Menace* (San Francisco: Jossey-Bass [1995], 2003).

5 end-of-the-world visions: Robert Jay Lifton, "The Image of 'The End of the World': A Psychohistorical View" in *Facing Apocalypse*, ed. Valerie Andrews, Robert Bosnak, and Karen Walter Goodwin (Dallas, Texas: Spring Publications, Inc., 1987).

5 "truly beautiful future for themselves": Stuart R. Schram, *Mao Tse-tung* (London: Penguin [1963], 1967).

6 Jeffrey Herf, a historian: Jeffery Herf, *Reactionary Modernism: Technology, Culture, and Politics in Weimar and the Third Reich* (Cambridge: Cambridge University Press, 1984).

7 "the last man to remain alive": Elias Canetti, *Crowds and Power* (New York: Viking, 1962).

9 nuclearism: Robert Jay Lifton, *The Broken Connection: On Death and the Continuity of Life* (Washington, DC: American Psychiatric Press [1979], 1996).

10 "fire and fury like the world has never seen": Peter Baker and Choe Sang-Hun, "Trump Threatens 'Fire and Fury' against North Korea if It Endangers U.S.," *New York Times*, August 8, 2017.

10 Trump has been inconsistent and contradictory: See Michael Lewis, "Why the Scariest Nuclear Threat May Be Coming from inside the White House," *Vanity Fair*, July 26, 2017.

11 "nuclear priesthood": See Steven Lee Myers, "Nuclear Priesthood Gets a New Credo," *New York Times*, December 14, 1997.

12 "living in truth": See Václav Havel, "The Power of the Powerless," in *Living in Truth* (London: Faber and Faber, 1987).

1: Chinese Communist Thought Reform

Excerpts are from: Robert Jay Lifton, *Thought Reform and the Psychology of Totalism: A Study of "Brainwashing" in China* (Chapel Hill: University of North Carolina Press [1961], 1989); *Witness to an Extreme Century: A Memoir* (New York: Free Press, 2011).

16 *"Let the hundred flowers bloom"*: See the pamphlets "Contradiction" and "The Storm" (China Viewpoints: Hong Kong, 1958); Benjamin Schwartz, "New Trends in Maoism," *Problems of Communism* 6 (1957):1–8.

18 the coerced bacteriological warfare confessions: A later study argued that America actually engaged in experimental biological warfare. Stephen Endicott and Edward Hagerman, *The United States and Biological Warfare: Secrets from the Early Cold War and Korea* (Bloomington and Indianapolis: Indiana University Press, 1998).

2: Revolutionary Immortality

Excerpt is from: Robert Jay Lifton, *Revolutionary Immortality: Mao Tse-tung and the Chinese Cultural Revolution* (New York: Norton Library [1968], 1976).

35 deaths of . . . three million people: See "The Cultural Revolution, 50 Years On: It Was the Worst of Times," *The Economist*, May 14, 2016.

36 astonishing number of deaths: See Frank Dikötter, *Mao's Great Famine: The History of China's Most Devastating Catastrophe, 1958–1962* (London: Bloomsbury [2010], 2017).

37 "Should the imperialists impose": Schram, *Mao Tse-tung*, 302.

38 Mao's personal physician: Dr. Li Zhisui, *The Private Life of Chairman Mao: The Memoirs of Mao's Personal Physician*, trans. Tai Hung-chao, ed. Anne F. Thurston (New York: Random House, 2011).

38 One observer summarizes Mao: Jonathan Mirsky, "Unmasking the Monster," *New York Review of Books*, November 17, 1994.

62 Chinese suppression of Falun Gong: J.Y., "What Is Falun Gong: China's Government Calls It an 'Evil Cult,'" *The Economist*, September 5, 2018. See also David Ownby, *Falun Gong and the Future of China* (New York: Oxford University Press [2008], 2010).

62 Tiananmen Square uprising: Liang Zhang, *The Tiananmen Papers*, ed. Andrew J. Nathan and Perry Link (New York: PublicAffairs, 2002).

63 Falun Gong was indeed a cult: See Cult Education Institute, "Falun Gong aka Falun Dafa," https://culteducation.com/group/1254-falun-gong.html.

63 2017 show trials of human rights lawyers and activists: Chris Buckley, "Activist Confesses to Subversion in Chinese Show Trial," *New York Times*, August 22, 2017.

64 Since 2016 . . . a million Uighurs: Eva Dou, Jeremy Page, and Josh Chin, "China's Uighur Camps Swell as Beijing Widens the Dragnet," *Wall Street Journal*, August 17, 2018.

64 "Cultural cleansing . . . final solution": Gerry Shih, "China's Mass-Indoctrination Camps Evoke Cultural Revolution," Associated Press, May 17, 2018.

65 "The Thought of Xi Jinping": Angela Stanzel et al., *China's 'New Era' with Xi Jinping Characteristics*, (London: European Council on Foreign Relations, 2017).

3: Ideological Totalism—the "Eight Deadly Sins"

Excerpt is from: Robert Jay Lifton, *Thought Reform and the Psychology of Totalism: A Study of "Brainwashing" in China* (Chapel Hill: University of North Carolina Press [1961], 1989).

4: On Cultism and the Larger Society

96 as a "higher purpose": Alex Inkeles, "The Totalitarian Mystique: Some Impressions of the Dynamics of Totalitarian Society," in *Totalitarianism*, ed. Carl Friedrich (Cambridge, MA: Harvard University Press, 1953), 88, 91.

97 a cult called Peoples Temple: See Robert Jay Lifton, *Destroying the World to Save It: Aum Shinrikyō, Apocalyptic Violence, and the New Global Terrorism* (New York: Metropolitan Books [1999], 2000); and Tim Reiterman, *Raven: The Untold Story of the Rev. Jim Jones and His People* (New York: Dutton, 1982).

99 came to be called "snapping": See Flo Conway and Jim Siegelman, *Snapping: America's Epidemic of Sudden Personality Change* (New York: Stillpoint Press, 1995).

99 what I have called "doubling": Lifton, *Nazi Doctors*, 118–29.

99 2018 Netflix television series . . . the Rajneeshees: *Wild Wild Country*, directed by Maclain Way and Chapman Way (Los Gatos, CA: Netflix, 2018). See also Sam Wolfson, "The Free-Love Cult That Terrorised America—and Became Netflix's Latest Must-Watch," *The Guardian*, April 7, 2018.

101 The term "fundamentalism": See Martin E. Marty, "Fundamentalism as a Social Phenomenon," *Bulletin of the American Academy of Arts and Sciences* 42 (1988): 15–29.

5: Aum Shinrikyō

Excerpt is from: Robert Jay Lifton, *Destroying the World to Save It: Aum Shinrikyō, Apocalyptic Violence, and the New Global Terrorism* (New York: Metropolitan Books [1999], 2000).

108 "forcing the end": Gershom Scholem, *The Messianic Idea in Judaism* (New York: Schocken, 1971), 56–57.

109 the lone survivor: Manabu Watanabe, one of Japan's leading scholars on Aum, pointed that out in his paper "Salvation of the Other in Aum Shinrikyō: An Impossible Endeavor," presented at the 1997

meeting of the International Association for Asian Philosophy and Religion, 12.

109 "the last man to remain alive": Elias Canetti, *Crowds and Power* (New York: Viking, 1962).

109 ISIS too takes a stand: William McCants, *The ISIS Apocalypse: The History, Strategy, and Doomsday Vision of the Islamic State* (London: St. Martin's Press, 2016).

109 they eventually did hang him: Austin Ramzy, "Japan Executes Cult Leader behind 1995 Sarin Gas Subway Attack," *New York Times*, July 5, 2018.

6: Nazi Doctors

Excerpt is from: Robert Jay Lifton, *The Nazi Doctors: Medical Killing and the Psychology of Genocide* (New York: Basic Books [1986], 2017).

134 Nazi millennialism: David Redles, *Hitler's Millennial Reich: Apocalyptic Belief and the Search for Salvation* (New York: New York University Press, 2008).

135 Raul Hilberg, the great Holocaust scholar: Raul Hilberg, *The Destruction of the European Jews* (New Haven: Yale University Press, 2003).

135 Hannah Arendt: Hannah Arendt, *Eichmann in Jerusalem: A Report on the Banality of Evil* (New York: The Viking Press, 1963).

135 the Nordic race alone: Adolf Hitler, *Mein Kampf* (Boston: Houghton Mifflin [1925–26], 1943).

135 "Of course I am a doctor": Dr. Ella Lingens-Reiner, recalling a conversation with Nazi doctor Fritz Klein. See also Lingens-Reiner, *Prisoners of Fear* (London: Gollancz, 1948), 1–2.

136 "life unworthy of life": Karl Binding and Alfred Hoche, *Die Freigabe der Vernichtung lebensunwerten Lebens* [The permission to destroy life unworthy of life] (Leipzig, Germany: F. Meiner, 1920).

137 his participation in the killing process: As far as I could learn there was only one female Nazi doctor assigned to Auschwitz, Herta Oberheuser. Since I was unable to talk to her, all of those I interviewed were men.

Notes

7: Trump

Excerpts are from: Robert Jay Lifton, "The Assault on Reality," *Dissent*, April 10, 2018; and Lifton, "When Trump's Spell Is Broken: What Do His Followers Do If It Turns Out He Can't Build the Wall?" *Daily News*, February 1, 2019.

153 "very stable genius": For Donald Trump's tweets, see Emily Stewart, "Trump Tweets That He's a Genius and 'a Very Stable Genius at That!,'" *Vox*, January 6, 2018.

153 he alone can "fix" . . . our society: Trump's GOP nomination speech, in Yoni Appelbaum, "I Alone Can Fix It," *The Atlantic*, July 21, 2016.

153 "deconstruction of the administrative state": Joshua Green, *Devil's Bargain: Steve Bannon, Donald Trump, and the Storming of the Presidency* (New York: Penguin, 2017).

153 group known as QAnon: See Jane Coaston, "#QAnon, the Scarily Popular Pro-Trump Conspiracy Theory, Explained," *Vox*, August 2, 2018; and Will Sommer, "What Is QAnon? The Craziest Theory of the Trump Era, Explained," *Daily Beast*, July 6, 2018.

155 the caravan in question: Bryan Mealer, "This Is What Trump's Caravan 'Invasion' Really Looks Like," *The Guardian*, November 26, 2018.

155 writings of psychological professionals: *The Dangerous Case of Donald Trump: 27 Psychiatrists and Mental Health Experts Assess a President*, ed. Bandy Lee (New York: Thomas Dunne Books, 2017).

158 The psychologist Jerome Bruner: Jerome Bruner, "The Narrative Construction of Reality," *Critical Inquiry* 18, no. 1 (1991): 1–21.

158 Todd Gitlin calls "The Vortex": Todd Gitlin, "Flat Earthers and Feedback Loops," BillMoyers.com, August 1, 2017.

159 "virtually indifferent to reality": David Leonhardt, Ian Prasad Philbrick, and Stuart A. Thompson, "Trump's Lies vs. Obama's," *New York Times Sunday Review*, December 14, 2017.

160 tendency in false confessions: Lifton, *Thought Reform*, 38–60.

161 Rush Limbaugh and Ann Coulter: Michael Brice-Saddler, "'This Is Tyranny of Talk Radio Hosts, Right?' Limbaugh and Coulter Blamed for Trump's Shutdown," *The Guardian*, December 22, 2018.

163 were quick to testify against him: Lifton, *Destroying the World to Save It*, 173–78.

164 "Cult of Kek": Jason Wilson, "Hiding in Plain Sight: How the 'Alt-Right' Is Weaponizing Irony to Spread Fascism," *The Guardian*, May 23, 2017; and Emma Grey Ellis, "Witches, Frog-Gods, and the Deepening Schism of Internet Religions," *Wired*, April 3, 2018.

165 "Bannon's arsenal of weaponry": Olivia Solon, "Cambridge Analytica Whistleblower Says Bannon Wanted to Suppress Voters," *The Guardian*, May 16, 2018.

165 The dirty tricks: Matthew Rosenberg, "Cambridge Analytica, Trump-Tied Political Firm, Offered to Entrap Politicians," *New York Times*, March 19, 2018.

165 Aleksandr Kogan: Carole Cadwalladr and Emma Graham-Harrison, "Cambridge Analytica: Links to Moscow Oil Firm and St Petersburg University," *The Guardian*, March 17, 2018; and Matthew Rosenberg, "Professor Apologizes for Helping Cambridge Analytica Harvest Facebook Data," *New York Times*, April 22, 2018.

166 "4 or 5 thousand data points": Tom Cheshire, "Behind the Scenes at Donald Trump's UK Digital War Room," *Sky News*, October 22, 2016.

166 the wild conspiracism: Russell Muirhead and Nancy Rosenblum, *A Lot of People Are Saying: The New Conspiracism and the Assault on Democracy* (Princeton and Oxford: Princeton University Press, 2019).

8: The Apocalyptic Twins: Nuclear and Climate Threats

168 these "apocalyptic twins": See Robert Jay Lifton, *The Climate Swerve: Reflections on Mind, Hope, and Survival* (New York: The New Press, 2017), 17–66.

168 Niels Bohr and Robert Oppenheimer: See Richard Rhodes, *The Making of the Atomic Bomb* (New York: Simon and Schuster [1986], 2012).

170 widespread psychic numbing: Lifton, *The Broken Connection*, 366–67.

170 one plane, one bomb, one city: Lifton, *Witness to an Extreme Century*, 112.

170 "Legacy of Hiroshima": Edward Teller with Allen Brown, *The Legacy of Hiroshima* (New York: Praeger, 1975), 180–81.

171 "In a sense the system built itself": Thomas Powers, "How Nuclear War Could Start," *New York Review of Books*, January 17, 1985, 35. See also Herbert York, *Race to Oblivion: A Participant's View of the Arms Race* (New York: Simon and Schuster, 1970), 228–32.

172 better termed "climate rejecters": Lifton, *The Climate Swerve*.

173 the Dark Mountain Project: For an article by its leader, see Paul Kingsnorth, "Why I Stopped Believing in Environmentalism and Started the Dark Mountain Project," *The Guardian*, April 29, 2010. See also Daniel Smith, "It's the End of the World as We Know It . . . and He Feels Fine," *New York Times*, April 17, 2014.

9: The Protean Alternative

Excerpt is from: Robert Jay Lifton, *The Protean Self: Human Resilience in an Age of Fragmentation* (New York: Basic Books, 1995).

177 put forward by Ernst Cassirer: See Cassirer, *An Essay on Man: An Introduction to a Philosophy of Human Culture* (New Haven, CT: Yale University Press [1944], 1962); and *The Philosophy of Symbolic Forms*, vol. 3, *The Phenomenology of Knowledge* (New Haven, CT: Yale University Press [1957], 1973).

178 "transformational nature of human nature": See Langer, *Philosophy in a New Key: A Study in the Symbolism of Reason, Rite, and Art* (New York: New American Library [1942], 1951); and her three-volume study, *Mind: An Essay on Human Feeling* (Baltimore, MD: Johns Hopkins Press, 1967–82).

178 "animating guilt": Robert Jay Lifton, *Home from the War: Learning from Vietnam Veterans* (New York: Other Press [1973], 2005).

10: Regaining Reality

189 malignant normality: Lifton, *The Nazi Doctors*, preface to the 2017 edition; and *The Climate Swerve*, 67–92.

190 "witnessing professionals": Lifton, *The Climate Swerve*, 93–100.

Notes

190 As Havel explained: Havel, "Power of the Powerless."

191 "experiments with truth": Mohandas K. Gandhi, *Autobiography: The Story of My Experiments with Truth* (New York: Dover [1948], 1983).

191 "Rather than . . . give me truth": *Thoreau's Political Writings*, ed. Nancy L. Rosenblum (Cambridge: Cambridge University Press, 1996).

192 the historian Richard Hofstadter: Richard Hofstadter, *The Paranoid Style in American Politics and Other Essays* (New York: Vintage Books, 1967).

Index

Aleph (Aum Shinrikyō), 110

antiwar veterans, 178

apocalypticism, 5–9; of Aum
    Shinrikyō, 107–9, 111–15,
    126, 131; in climate change,
    11, 172–74; of ISIS, 109–10;
    in Nazism, 134; nuclear
    weapons in, 9, 10; in
    Trump's oratory, 153

Applewhite, Marshall Herff, 133

Arendt, Hannah, 135

Aum Shinrikyō, 2, 7, 96;
    apocalypticism of, 5–6, 107–15;
    crosses threshold to forcing
    Armageddon, 125–31; guruism
    of, 116–19; initiations into,
    120–22; ISIS compared
    with, 109–10; nuclearism
    of, 10; *shukke* in, 119–20;
    symbolizing by, 178;
    violence of, 98

Auschwitz (death camp, Poland),
    135, 137; doctor-supervised
    killings at, 144–47, 189;
    survivors of, 178–79, 191

Bannon, Steve, 153, 165

Barr, William, 155

biological mysticism, 6, 7, 141–42

biology: in Nazi ideology, 134–36,
    147; in Nazi imagery, 139;
    of symbolism, 178

bioterrorism: by Aum Shinrikyō, 107,
    110, 114; by Rajneeshees, 100

Bohr, Niels, 168–69

brainwashing, 17–18

Bruner, Jerome, 158

Buber, Martin, 89, 126

Buddhism, 112, 129

Cambridge Analytica (firm), 165, 166

Camus, Albert, 76, 79, 85, 88

Cassirer, Ernst, 177–78

China: Falun Gong in, 62–63;
    Great Proletarian Cultural
    Revolution in, 34–41, 48–52;
    Mao myth tied to, 54–56;
    nuclear weapons developed
    by, 9; Red Guards in, 45–48;
    Soviet Union compared with,
    90; Uighur Muslims in, 64–65

Chinese Communist Party: Falun
    Gong and, 62–63; Great
    Proletarian Cultural Revolution
    and, 34–37, 39; Hundred
    Flowers Movement and, 16,
    31–32; Mao's founding of,
    42; milieu control by, 69

Index

Chinese communist thought reform, 2–3, 15–17; brainwashing and, 17–18; of Chinese intellectuals, 24–27; of Chinese population, 19–21; filial piety as target of, 26–29; Great Proletarian Cultural Revolution and, 34, 35; ideological totalism of, 67–68; during Korean War, 18–19; persistence of, 61–65; in prisons, 22–24; responses to, 30–33

Christianity: fundamentalism in, 101–2

climate change, 172–74; apocalypticism in, 11

Clinton, Bill, 184

Clinton, Hillary, 153, 156–57

confessions, 19, 74–75; by Chinese intellectuals, 24–25; by Chinese prisoners, 23; cult of, 76–79; false, 160

Confucianism, 26–28, 96

Confucius, 29, 65

conspiracies, 164–65

Coulter, Ann, 161

Cox, Harvey, 4

cult of confessions, 76–79

cult of enthusiasm, 29

"Cult of Kek," 164

cult of personality, 56–57

cultism, 92–103, 172–173, 179; concept of, 2–4; in Communist China, 3, 39; Nazis and, 6, 134, 136–37, 140; nuclear weapons and, 10–11; reactionary, 12; Trump and, 152–53, 161

cults, 2–4; and eight deadly sins, 66; Falun Gong as, 63; origins of word, 95, 97; radicalism and reaction of, 101; social context of, 94–95; totalism in, 67–68; use of terms, 4–5; violence tied to, 97–100

Cultural Revolution (China), 34–41, 44, 61; Maoist thought in, 50–52; purity and power in, 48–49

cyanide, 98

Czechoslovakia, 185, 190–91

Dark Mountain Project (organization), 173, 174

death and rebirth (symbolic), 23–24; symbolic immortality and, 40–44

demand for purity, 73–76

deprogrammers, 94

dispensing of existence, 87–90

doctors: Auschwitz survivors, 178–79; Nazi, 137–47

doctrine: primacy of, 83–86

Doniger, Wendy, 126

"doubling," 145–46

eight deadly sins, 66; cult of confession in, 76–79; demand for purity as, 73–76; dispensing of existence as, 87–90; loading language as, 81–83; milieu control as, 68–71; mystical manipulation as, 71–73; primacy of doctrine in, 83–86; sacred science as, 79–81

Erikson, Erik, 191

euthanasia: by Nazis, 143–44

existence, dispensing of, 87–90

Facebook, 165–66

Fairbank, John K., 84

Falun Gong, 62–63

filial piety, 26–29

Index

First World War, 149
Flat Earth Cult, 172
Foster, Vince, 158
fundamentalism, 101–2, 182–83

Gandhi, Mohandas, 191–92
generational struggles, 26
genocide, 6; by Nazis, 147–48, 150–51
Germany: in First World War, 149; as Weimar Republic, 148
Gitlin, Todd, 158
global warming, 172–74
Gogol, Nikolai, 26
Graham, Lindsey, 162
Great Leap Forward (China), 35–36, 43; psychism in, 59
Great Proletarian Cultural Revolution (China). *See* Cultural Revolution
guilty milieu, 74–75
gurus and guruism: in Aum Shinrikyō, 119–22, 125–26; in Hinduism, 118; Mao as, 36–37; mentors distinguished from, 11; as part of divine purification plan, 7; Shōkō Asahara as, 116–17, 119, 122–23; Trump as, 152–53; violence used by, 98

Havel, Václav, 190–92
Heaven's Gate (cult), 133
Herf, Jeffrey, 6
Hideo Murai, 119
Hilberg, Raul, 135
Hinduism: gurus in, 118; Shiva myth in, 126–27
Hiroshima (Japan), 10, 108, 170, 178
Hitler, Adolf, 135, 150; in First World War, 149; as guru, 134; *Mein Kampf* by, 138–40; new

bureaucracy created by, 142; Shōkō Asahara's admiration of, 108; suicide of, 151
Hofstadter, Richard, 192
Hong Kong, 16
hubris, 88
human experience: subordination to doctrine of, 83–84
Hundred Flowers Movement (China), 16, 31–32

ideological totalism, 1–2, 67–68, 90–93; eight deadly sins of, 66; Trump as antithesis of, 156
internet: social media on, 164–67
Islamic State (ISIS), 109–10

James, William, 132
Japan: apocalypticism in culture of, 113; atomic bombs used against, 170; Aum Shinrikyō in, 109; post-Hiroshima culture of, 10
Jews: killed at Auschwitz, 135, 136; killed by Nazis, 143–44; Nazi ideology on, 139–40
Jones, Alex, 165
Jones, Jim, 97–98, 133

Kek, Cult of, 164
Khomeini, Ruhollah (Ayatollah), 182, 187–88
Khrushchev, Nikita, 56, 57
Kierkegaard, Søren, 148
Kim Jong-un, 10
Kingsnorth, Paul, 173–74
Kogan, Aleksandr, 165–66
Korean War, 18–19

Index

Langer, Susanne K., 177–78
language: loading of, 81–83
Leonhardt, David, 159
Li Hongzhi, 62, 63
Limbaugh, Rush, 161
Lin Biao, 53–54
loading language, 81–83
Los Alamos (New Mexico), 168
Lu Xun, 26

malignant normality, 189–90
Manson, Charles, 133
Maoists and Maoism: in Cultural
    Revolution thought, 50–52;
    on nuclear weapons, 9;
    sacralization of Mao's thoughts
    in, 52–54; of Xi Jinping, 65
Mao Zedong, 2; admired by Shōkō
    Asahara, 108; apocalypticism
    of, 5, 37–38; Chinese thought
    reform tied to, 3; evocation of
    "people" by, 7; Great Proletarian
    Cultural Revolution under,
    34–39, 50–51; hero myth of,
    54–56; on nuclear weapons,
    9, 171; psychism of, 58–61; on
    punishment and cure, 21; Red
    Guard and, 47–49; sacralization
    of thoughts of, 52–54, 57–58;
    in Schurmann film, 46–47;
    Snow interview with, 41–42;
    symbolic immortality of, 42–44
Matsumoto (Japan), 114
McCarthy, Joseph, 17
McCarthyism, 16–17
Mein Kampf (Hitler), 139–40
mentors, 11
Mercer, Robert, 165
milieu control, 68–71

Mueller, Robert, 153, 154
mystical manipulation, 71–73
mysticism: in Nazi ideology, 141

Nagasaki (Japan), 170
narcissism, 156
nationalism, 150, 182
Nazism and Nazis, 134–37; and
    biological mysticism, 6, 7,
    141–42; gas chambers of, 98;
    genocide by, 147–48, 150–51;
    malignant normality of, 189; Nazi
    doctors, 137–47; "reactionary
    modernism" in, 6; Riefenstahl
    films of, 46; Volk concept in, 7
"new religions," 4
Nix, Alexander, 165, 166
North Korea, 10
nuclearism, 9–10, 168–71; in Aum
    Shinrikyō, 128–29; Mao and,
    9, 37, 171; Trump and, 10
nuclear priesthood, 11, 169, 171
nuclear war: in Aum Shinrikyō
    beliefs, 108–9; fundamentalism
    and, 101–2; Mao on, 5, 37
nuclear weapons, 9–11, 184; in Aum
    Shinrikyō ideology, 128–29; Aum
    Shinrikyō's attempt to obtain,
    107, 114; China's development
    of, 53; development of, 168–71;
    Maoist thought on, 60–61

Obama, Barack, 153, 160
Oppenheimer, Robert, 168–69
organ donations, in China, 62
Orwell, George, 68–69

Peking University, 45
people and nonpeople, 87–89

Index

Peoples Temple (cult), 97–98, 133
Perot, Ross, 184
poa (Buddhist belief), 112, 127
Poland, 191
politics: apocalypticism in, 5;
 totalism in, 67–68
postmodernism, 186–87
power: in Cultural Revolution, 48–49
prisons and prisoners: in China,
 22–24; milieu control in, 69
proteanism, 4, 11–12, 177–79;
 protean self, 179–88
Proteus (deity), 179
psychism, 58–61
psychohistorical dislocation, 100–101
psychoses, 8, 159
purging milieu, 76
purity (purification): in Aum
 Shinrikyō ideology, 128; in
 Cultural Revolution, 48–49;
 demand for, 73–76; in Mao, 50;
 in Nazi ideology, 141, 150, 151

QAnon (group), 153–54, 164

Rajneeshees (cult), 100
Rank, Otto, 147–48
reactionary modernism, 6
reality: loss of, 179, 192; ownership of,
 7–8; Trump's assault on, 156–61
Red Guards (China), 34–36,
 39, 45–49, 57
re-education, 19; of Chinese prisoners,
 23; of Uighur Muslims, 64
religion: apocalypticism in, 5,
 126; fundamentalism in,
 101–2, 182–83; in origin of
 cults, 95; totalism in, 67–68
revolutionary romanticism, 55

revolutionary universities, 25–26;
 milieu control in, 69
Rhodes, Richard, 168–69
Riefenstahl, Leni, 46
Roosevelt, Franklin D., 170
Rushdie, Salman, 182, 187–88
Russia, 165–66

sacred science, 79–81; language for,
 82
Sapir, Edward, 82
sarin (poison gas), 110, 114
The Satanic Verses (Rushdie), 182
Scholem, Gershom, 108
Schram, Stuart, 56
Schurmann, Franz, 46–47
Schwartz, Benjamin, 85
science and scientists: in Aum
 Shinrikyō ideology, 130–31; in
 development of nuclear weapons,
 168–71; in Nazi ideology, 6, 147;
 recruited by Aum Shinrikyō,
 119
shaming milieu, 74–75
Shigeo Sugimoto, 124
Shiva (deity), 126–27
Shōkō Asahara, 10; apocalypticism of,
 107–8, 111–15; arrest and trial of,
 123–24, 163; execution of, 109; as
 guru of Aum Shinrikyō, 116–21;
 megalomania of, 122–23, 125–27
shukke (monks or nuns), 119–21
Singer, Margaret, 4
"snapping" (quick reversion of cult
 members to pre-cult identity),
 99
Snow, Edgar, 41–42, 56
social media, 164–67
solipsistic reality, 156, 159–61

Index

Soros, George, 153
Soviet Union: breakup of, 184;
    China compared with, 90;
    under Khrushchev, 56, 57
Speer, Albert, 150–51
Stalin, Josef, 56–57
sterilizations, by Nazis, 142–43
Stern, Fritz, 148
Storr, Anthony, 117
Stunkard, Albert, 136
symbolic forms, 177
symbolic immortality, 40–44
symbolization, 177–78

technology: apocalypticism through,
    9; in Aum Shinrikyō ideology,
    130; psychism and, 59–61; in
    stemming climate change, 173–74
Teller, Edward, 170
Thoreau, Henry David, 191–92
thought reform: milieu control
    in, 68–71. See also Chinese
    Communist thought reform
Tibetan Book of the Dead, 118
Tokyo (Japan), 114
totalism, 90–93, 181–82; Trump
    as antithesis of, 156. See also
    ideological totalism
transcendence, experiences of, 153
Trilling, Lionel, 82
Trump, Donald, 152–55, 189, 192;
    assault on reality by, 156–61;
    on attacking North Korea, 10;

loyal base support for, 161–64;
    social media used by, 164–67
Twitter, 165

Uighur Muslims (China), 64–65
ultimate weapons, 128–29
United States: cults in, 132–33;
    malignant normality in, 189;
    McCarthyism in, 16–17

Vajrayana, 129
Velvet Revolution
    (Czechoslovakia), 190–91
veterans, antiwar, 178
violence of cults, 97–100; by Aum
    Shinrikyō, 107, 110, 112; in Aum
    Shinrikyō ideology, 127; in Aum
    Shinrikyō initiations, 122
Volk (people), 7, 140, 146

wandering zealots, 36
Weaver, Richard, 82
Wright, Mary C., 84

Xi Jinping, 65

Yoshihiro Inoue, 124

zealotry, 11–12; psychology of, 66–67;
    totalism and,
    67–68
Zyklon B (gas used in gas
    chambers), 98